DYING TO BE HAPPY

CHRIS STEPIEN

Dying

TO BE

Happy

Discovering
THE TRUTH
About
LIFE

BEACON

Scripture texts in this work are taken from the *New American Bible, revised
edition* © 2010, 1991, 1986, 1970 Confraternity of Christian Doctrine,
Washington, D.C., and are used by permission of the copyright owner. All
rights reserved. No part of the *New American Bible* may be reproduced in
any form without permission in writing from the copyright owner.

Note: The stories in this book are true. In some cases, names have been
changed and details omitted to protect the anonymity of private individuals.

Cover design: Leah Nienas
Interior: Finer Points Productions

ISBN: 978-1-942611-62-2 (hard cover)
ISBN: 978-1-942611-63-9 (soft cover)

Library of Congress Cataloging-in-Publication Data

Names: Stepien, Chris, author.
Title: Dying to be happy : discovering the truth about life / Chris Stepien.
Description: North Palm Beach, FL : Beacon Pub., 2016. | Includes bibliographical references.
Identifiers: LCCN 2016014042 (print) | LCCN 2016014454 (ebook) |
ISBN 9781942611622 (hardcover) | ISBN 9781942611639 (softcover) |
ISBN 9781942611646 (ebook)
Subjects: LCSH: Happiness--Religious aspects--Christianity. |
Death--Religious aspects--Christianity. | Life--Religious aspects--Christianity.
Classification: LCC BV4647.J68 S745 2016 (print) | LCC BV4647.J68 (ebook) |
DDC 233--dc23

2016014042

Printed in the United States of America [1]

To my darling Ellen,
Thank God he brought us together—for life.

Contents

Preface ix

ONE   You Fool 1

TWO   The Master of the House 7

THREE   The Sheep and the Goats Clause 13

FOUR   I Do What I Hate 21

FIVE   Drinking Poison 35

SIX   Lady Poverty 43

SEVEN   Let's Be Frank 55

EIGHT   Cards for Lazarus 64

NINE   Puff of Smoke 77

TEN   The Dash between the Dates 95

Postscript 107

Acknowledgments 109

Notes 111

About the Author 117

Preface

"I'll keep you in my prayers."

That promise is often a sign of trouble. The mere whiff of death has a way of making people more serious about faith. Hospitalization and surgeries, depression and suicides, exotic medical treatments, car crashes, falls, aging, pain, and difficult diseases are the seeds and fertilizer for genuine prayer.

Pleas for healing and miracles fill social media pages, e-mail prayer chains, and long lists of Mass intentions.

On the other hand, some people beg for death to come—now.

Let's not forget we're all dying every day. Today you're as young as you'll ever be. This could be your last sunrise or sunset.

How tight are you with your Maker?

If God calls your name before you turn this page, will you be ready for your homecoming?

Your happiness is in your dying hands.

ONE

You Fool

November 24, 2014

My wife has breast cancer.

It's aggressive. We're waiting for the surgeon at the university cancer center. It's Monday of Thanksgiving week, and the oncologist has just left the room. It turns out there is a new treatment strategy, and it doesn't matter whether Ellen has a mastectomy or undergoes chemotherapy first. But time is of the essence. So she'll have her right breast removed just before Christmas and start the New Year with a steady diet of poison plus cancer drugs. The medication will continue for a full year, long after the four months of chemo are done, most likely pouring through a port at the top of her chest right above her heart. Cardiac damage is one of the drug's potential side effects.

"I can almost certainly guarantee you will *not* have nausea and vomiting," said the physician with assurance. "But I *can* definitely guarantee you will lose your hair."

Truthfully, this respected and caring expert couldn't be certain of any outcome—except that Ellen will die. But it may not be the cancer that kills her. She might trip on her shoelace and sustain a head injury in the hospital parking garage. Or be crushed in a rollover crash on our way home when the driver of a semitrailer loses control of his rig in the windblown rain. Or my lovely wife may simply never wake up after we kiss goodnight and doze off.

Perhaps it will be my soul that slips away in the dark, while Ellen goes on to live twenty years without me.

Only one thing is certain. Guaranteed. No one is getting out of this life alive. We just hate to admit it. Is that because it's frightening? Unknowable?

Have you bought life insurance? Completed your will? Pre-planned your funeral? Staked out a cemetery plot? Maybe.

But have you thought much about judgment day?

Why is it easier to forget or procrastinate than prepare for our appointment with the grim reaper and our Creator?

Jesus frequently reminded his contemporaries of their death denial. One of his parables features a rich landowner who reaped an unusually abundant harvest. He knocked down his barns and built new, bigger silos to store up his huge surplus. The fortunate farmer made plans to party and live carefree, thanks to his newfound wealth. However, the Lord provided a surprise twist to teach the harsh truth about life.

> God said to him, "You fool, this night your life will be de-manded of you; and the things you have prepared, to whom will they belong? Thus will it be for the one who stores up treasure for himself but is not rich in what matters to God." (Luke 12:20–21)

We are going to die. Don't ever forget it. Our stay here is temporary. While we're alive, our mission is to serve God. That is what lasts forever.

Even the prayer Jesus taught his disciples reminds us of our mortality. "Give us this day our *daily* bread . . ."

Not an annual harvest. Not a monthly allowance, not even a week's worth. Just food for today. Enough to get by, from sunrise to sunset. Tomorrow is not included. And you're not entitled to it, no matter how convinced you are you'll pass that momentous milestone; ace that entrance exam; win the big game; throw the party of a lifetime; buy your dream house; watch your kids grow up, or play with your grandchildren and see them graduate.

We cannot earn these things; no matter how hard we work, study, diet, exercise, and invest to secure their likelihood. They are blessings, not dividends. Yet we often obsess about building enough wealth or making provisions to insure future plans.

"Don't worry about tomorrow," the Lord advises. Today offers enough to keep us busy, especially if we're truly living in the moment. Besides, "Can any of you by worrying add a single moment to your life-span?" Jesus asks in Matthew 6:27.

"Therefore I tell you, do not worry about your life, what you will eat (or drink), or about your body, what you will wear. Is not life more than food and the body more than clothing?" (Matthew 6:25)

Of course, it is. And anxiety doesn't lengthen life. In fact, worrying tends to shorten it and make the days we have miserable and our nights sleepless.

"If you worry, why pray? And if you pray, why worry?" Those are the words of a poor grandmother as she faced serious surgery for a disfiguring and disabling condition. The woman had just opened her home to her underemployed son, his wife, and young family. She was uncertain how things would play out, but she was willing to leave them in God's hands.

Have you ever gone to great efforts to make a series of backup plans, only to have the original arrangements go just fine? Or better yet, planned for every contingency and then have the event cancelled? How often do the things you worry about come true? How often do wonderful surprises occur in your life? Do you ever get the feeling that you're blessed by divine intervention? That you've got a friend upstairs? You do.

Moral of the story: we're not in control. God is. Forget that and we'll lose our way and our lives to fear and anxiety. Those are evil, diabolical forces. When we give in to them, we tell God we don't trust him to take care of us.

Then why do we believers worry so much? What do *you* worry about? How much time do you waste by stressing?

Why do we overthink, over-plan, overwork, over-buy, over-tweet, over-like, overcook, over-stock? Is it because we're afraid there won't be enough for tomorrow? Do we think the store is going to run out of fashions, food, or drinks? Why do we save for a distant future that may never come? Why do we fund a life expectancy that assumes we'll need premium long-term care?

The answer: We want to feel in control. We're afraid of things we can't control, despite the fact that with the Our Father we pray, "For *thine* is the kingdom, the power and the glory, now and forever. Amen." That's *thine,* not *mine.*

It is, indeed, hard to trust these words and put our complete faith in God. But is it really easier to play God than to trust him? To deny our mortality and convince ourselves that we can cover all the bases, insure all outcomes, spare no expense, leave no stone unturned—all in the name of preserving our earthy lives at all costs?

The irony is that many of the old and ailing pray for death. They long for the end of loneliness, suffering, drug interaction, interminable doctor appointments, tests, pain, and decay. Some accept the futility of delaying the inevitable. Wives pray to die before their husbands and vice versa.

Be careful what you wish for. Old age is not for the faint of heart. Trust the Lord. The Father knows best. Live to serve God, and let him manage the rest. Including the day you'll die.

He does anyway.

Unless a grain of wheat falls to the ground and dies, it remains just a grain of wheat; but if it dies, it produces much fruit. Whoever loves his life loses it, and whoever hates his life in this world will preserve it for eternal life. (John 12:24–25)

Are you ready to die if Jesus comes knocking today? Tonight? Not sure?

Fortunately there *may* still be time to prepare for our afterlife. And the first step is to recognize that the moment we're born we begin dying.

This should be top of mind for Catholics, or anyone who's ever thrown or watched a "Hail Mary" pass. ". . . Now and at the hour of our death. Amen." That hour could be now.

Death is as much a part of life as breathing, or eating, or celebrating a baptism or a birthday. Have you ever witnessed a death? Held someone's hand as he or she breathed his or her last? Unfortunately the irrational fear of death and its inevitability leads to so much of our misery. Jesus died for us so we can live forever, so we can be happy now and for eternity.

And yet we're chasing the delusion that happiness, peace, and security are hiding somewhere among earthly things. Madison Avenue invites us to "open happiness," and buy "happy meals." Meanwhile, a top-tier business school offers a master's level marketing course called "Designing (for) Delight," where you can learn to design happiness and spread happiness with happy brands.

But St. Paul the apostle says we'll only find true joy when we let go of this world and hold onto God for dear life. "The concern of the flesh is death, but the concern of the spirit is life and peace" (Romans 8:6).

Death versus life.

Worry versus peace.

Delusion versus truth.

Obsession versus trust.

Fear versus happiness.

Which side are you on?

By the way, all our planning for my wife's breast cancer treatment was for naught. As Christmas approached, yet another change of plans occurred. Ellen's sentinel lymph node biopsy was negative. It was very likely the cancer had not spread!

Her surgeons delayed the mastectomy until mid-January. At first we were a little scared. *Let's kill the cancer now!* we thought. But the doctors assured us the brief delay was medically safe. So, instead of the low-key Christmas we'd planned, we had three festive celebrations with our family. We also learned we would become grandparents in the coming year. We felt incredibly blessed.

Thank God. There's no need to worry. He is so merciful.

Trust him. He knows we're all dying to be happy.

TWO

The Master of the House

Irene was just ten years old when the tanks and troops rolled through her Polish village. Death became a daily companion.

She had already witnessed two of her brothers succumb to childhood illnesses before they reached the age of two. But the Nazis seemed more vicious than disease; they machine-gunned children; they shoved Lugers against the heads of those who hesitated when given a direct order. Foreign soldiers played cards at Irene's kitchen table, boozing while ogling the young, single girls who scurried to fetch food on demand. Many times Nazis slaughtered an entire family for concealing just one Jewish neighbor. Even cutting down a Christmas tree on your own farm could trigger an arrest.

The Gestapo liked to make examples of people who didn't obey their rules. They were in control of your country. Your property. Your life. Or so they believed.

They wielded the weapon of fear. And fear has the chilling ability to shackle the fearful. Some nights Irene and her family would sleep in the woods along the riverbank, hiding from invading soldiers who might raid their home. They could hear the voices of Germans, Russians, Mongolians, and the Polish underground echo through the trees, along the San River on the eastern edge of Poland.

It was a brisk fall day, and trouble was in the air. The warnings spread like fire in a dry hay barn. The underground had ambushed German troops the night before, and the Gestapo was seeking swift revenge. It was time to send a clear message.

When Irene got word that the enemy was coming, she was in the kitchen of her mother's farmhouse. Her father had died just before the war.

"Run now!" her aunt screamed, as she raced through the house and bolted out the door.

With no time to grab a coat, young Irene instinctively yanked the kitchen tablecloth and wrapped it around her shoulders as she scampered toward the small family forest. It was her best hope to escape the SS. The cloth was French with large, colorful blue checks. Her parents had bought it while working factory jobs in Revin, a little industrial town northeast of Paris. Irene was born there in 1928. That was a happy time, and those memories were true family treasures.

As she sprinted through the small peasant homestead, the farm girl spotted a laughable scene—a very large woman climbing up a small pine tree, hoping to hide in its branches.

Find a bigger tree, Irene thought as she ran for her life. For a brief instant she was able to escape the sheer terror of Nazi brutality by spotting humor in the horror.

But then, instantly, reality came roaring back as she approached the forest.

Zing! Zing! Zing! Bullets whizzed past her ears.

Would she be shot? Would the Nazis's dogs attack her? Would she die in a concentration camp?

Irene dove for the turf. It wasn't long before the Gestapo nabbed the young girl and many of her neighbors before they could reach the stand of trees. The German troops were justifiably hesitant to enter the woods, where underground marksmen would likely be waiting.

These menacing invaders in their black uniforms, adorned with skulls and swastikas, hustled the Poles into the tiny village square. Irene avoided eye contact, staring at the knee-high black boots the SS soldiers wore. They planned to load the captives onto a train headed for a work camp. The aggressive raid produced a crowd of prisoners. There were so many that some of them spilled off the village road into the drainage ditches as they walked their death march toward the railroad.

Irene's mind was spinning. But on that terrifying day in a tiny peasant town, the hand of God intervened. Just before the Nazis forced their civilian prisoners onto railroad cars, they permitted local families to bring the captives a meal. Irene's mother, Anna, and several relatives rushed to her aid.

"Take that tablecloth off your shoulders," Anna said. She bundled the cloth as if to cover the food they had brought and stuffed it into her daughter's arms. Then the family surrounded Irene and began to slowly walk away with her, as if she had simply come to share a morsel with the captured. It worked! They escaped. Her aunt, the one who had run through Irene's home shouting a desperate warning, also survived by hiding in an empty barrel inside a neighbor's mudroom. And believe it or not, somehow the Nazis overlooked the large, round woman in the little pine tree. Perhaps the Lord had shrouded her under his pinions while the rest of the captured boarded the death train.

Jesus would not call Irene home the next day either. In fact, she would survive the war, marry, bear three sons and one daughter, and become an American citizen, a grandmother, and great-grandmother many times over.

I am Irene's third child, and her war stories always mesmerized me. My late father, Ludwik, was eight years older than my mother, and he had many similar experiences, including having the barrel of a submachine gun shoved under his chin by an impatient Nazi who wanted more information. In some ways, their survival was biblical. As Jesus said:

> Two men will be out in the field; one will be taken, and one will be left. Two women will be grinding at the mill; one will be taken, and one will be left. Therefore, stay awake! For you do not know on which day your Lord will come. (Matthew 24:40–42)

Although he was speaking of his second coming, the Lord's advice is priceless for daily life and our acceptance of death. You can't really begin to live without embracing it.

If you knew you were going to die today . . .

What would you do?

What would you do first?

Who would you tell?

What would you say?

Would you pray?

For whom would you pray?

Who would you call or visit?

Where would you go?

Who would you thank?

To whom would you give a heartfelt apology?

Who would you forgive?

Would you go to confession? Mass?

Who would you hug?

Who would you help?

What would you eat and drink?

Who would you feed?

Would you gamble?

Would you watch the game? Go fishing?

Would you tune in the news?

How much time would you spend on politics?

What would you do with your wealth and possessions?

What is the last thing you'd like to say?

So what are you waiting for? None of us knows how long we will live. But we all know we will die. It's just a question of when, where, and how.

Be sure of this: if the master of the house had known the hour of night when the thief was coming, he would have stayed awake and not let his house be broken into. So too, you also must be prepared, for at an hour you do not expect, the Son of Man will come. (Matthew 24:43–44)

These are the words of everlasting life—a new life we can begin today!

THREE

The Sheep and the Goats Clause

Iconic country music star Tim McGraw won a Grammy in 2004 for his performance of "Live Like You Were Dying." The two song-smiths who penned the tune, Craig Wiseman and Tim Nichols, told music biographer Jake Brown they were inspired by true stories about people who had a brush with a deadly diagnosis or battled terminal illness and decided to seize each day instead of throwing a self-pity party.[1] The advice of their simple words is profound, especially for those who have not yet had the benefit of a health scare.

Perhaps you heard McGraw's song and thought, *I should do that. Stop and smell the roses. Imitate the spirit of the movie* Ferris Bueller's Day Off. *Give my wife or husband a second kiss before I go out the door. Call Mom, Dad, or Grandpa just for fun. Buy my old friend lunch and let that grudge go. Shower my boss or teacher with kindness.*

Those are all good ideas. And like the lyrics in McGraw's ballad, they'd sound even nicer with music and a chorus of backup singers. It's a grand ole gospel of goodness and gratitude that, if followed, can help lead us to some serenity in the here and now. "Live Like You Were Dying" was so popular it led to an inspirational book by the same name that became a *New York Times* best seller.

But Jesus always raises the bar on any gospel. After all, he's focused on forever. Christianity demands much more of us than checking off our bucket list, reading our Bible, being kind and ending a few family feuds. In fact, the Lord gave us a virtual legal contract for what it takes to really live well in this world—to die to sin and gain eternal life in the kingdom of God.

I call it "The Sheep and the Goats Clause." It's all laid out in Matthew 25. When was the last time you read it? Not lately? Well, since it contains the terms and conditions for your heavenly mansion, it deserves at least as much attention as your mortgage, bank statement, student loan, or homework assignment.

It will only take a few minutes to carefully review the Lord's pact. There's no fine print. Jesus offers an ironclad contract for what he expects of us before we die. In addition to practicing as the divine physician, he would have made the ultimate savvy lawyer. See if you can find any loopholes. Good luck, because I can't.

The Sheep and the Goats Clause: The Judgment of the Nations

"When the Son of Man comes in his glory, and all the angels with him, he will sit upon his glorious throne, and all the nations will be assembled before him. And he will separate them one from another, as a shepherd separates the sheep from the goats. He will place the sheep on his right and the goats on his left.

Then the king will say to those on his right, 'Come, you who are blessed by my Father. Inherit the kingdom prepared for you from the foundation of the world. For I was hungry and you gave me food, I was thirsty and you gave me drink, a stranger and you welcomed me, naked and you clothed me, ill and you cared for me, in prison and you visited me.'

Then the righteous will answer him and say, 'Lord, when did we see you hungry and feed you, or thirsty and give you drink? When did we see you a stranger and welcome you, or naked and clothe you? When did we see you ill or in prison, and visit you?'

And the king will say to them in reply, 'Amen, I say to you, whatever you did for one of these least brothers of mine, you did for me.'

Then he will say to those on his left, 'Depart from me, you accursed, into the eternal fire prepared for the devil and his angels. For I was hungry and you gave me no food, I was thirsty and you gave me no drink, a stranger and you gave me no welcome, naked and you gave me no clothing, ill and in prison, and you did not care for me.'

Then they will answer and say, 'Lord, when did we see you hungry or thirsty or a stranger or naked or ill or in prison, and not minister to your needs?' He will answer them, 'Amen, I say to you, what you did not do for one of these least ones, you did not do for me.' And these will go off to eternal punishment, but the righteous to eternal life." (Matthew 25:31–46)

Are you feeling sheepish? Got wool? Will you smell like a lamb or a kid goat on judgment day?

As you just read, not only does our Lord tell us exactly what to do—he also tells us the consequences of complacency and inaction. The Bible is much more than a rulebook about what to avoid; Jesus spells out what is unavoidable. Christianity is not just a way of life or a path to follow. It must define our very essence, the shape of our footprints.

It's a freedom march for love and justice, a revolution against the sins of self-centeredness, apathy, greed, and pride. It's a revolt against our very human nature in order to become like God and live in his image and likeness. It requires impassioned believers, true rebels who are willing to give up the meaningless indulgences of this world to bring heaven to earth. And that takes both words and deeds, large and small, most done quietly.

Now how do you feel about passing that homeless beggar again today? Do you have anything to share? At least a smile and some conversation? A sandwich? Maybe a gift certificate for the grocery store or the local diner?

Did you visit or call your niece when she was in jail or rehab?

When you're at the water cooler or online, what do you say about immigrants? How about people of different races and religions?

When your brother faced divorce, did you judge him? Or did you bite your tongue and offer your shoulder to cry on for a while?

Have you ever made friends with a poor person?

Were you the first or last to welcome the new family to the neighborhood?

Have you called your grandparents recently? Visited them? What about your elderly aunt, uncle, or neighbor?

How long did you stay at the funeral home when your cousin, the recluse, died? Did you pray for him when he was sick?

Did you offer the Muslim woman your seat on the bus? Do you pray for a peaceful solution to terrorism?

How often do you donate to the church poor boxes? Do you contribute groceries to the local food bank?

What about that guy you see walking home from church? Have you ever offered him a ride?

How worn were the items you gave to the clothing drive?

In a word, Matthew 25 is about mercy. St. James agrees: "For the judgment is merciless to one who has not shown mercy; mercy triumphs over judgment" (James 2:13).

Whew! Thanks to God's mercy, there's hope for us after all.

The meaning of the word *mercy*, now a synonym for *compassion*, was shaped by several languages. Early Christians used the Latin word *merces* or "wages." They adapted it to describe the spiritual rewards a person received for an act of kindness—when performed in response to an unkind act. Later, in early French, the word became *merci* or *mercit*. Appropriately, among French speakers *merci* has evolved to mean "thank you."[2] God wants us to express our gratitude to him by being compassionate to others. Love your neighbor. Especially the one who is suffering.

Jesus said, "When you hold a banquet, invite the poor, the crippled, the lame, the blind; blessed indeed will you be because of their inability to repay you. For you will be repaid at the resurrection of the righteous" (Luke 14:13–14).

Blessed Teresa of Calcutta, known worldwide as Mother Teresa, personified the teachings in Matthew 25 and dined with the forgotten masses. Her tireless service to the poorest of the poor was her way of constantly preaching the gospel. Spanish journalist José Luis González-Balado captured a lifetime of her wisdom on the subject of love and mercy in his book *Mother*

Teresa: In My Own Words. No spoiler alert necessary; her insights are unvarnished.

"Do you not believe that it can happen . . . that we treat the poor like they are a garbage bag in which we throw everything we have no use for?" she asked. "Food we do not like or that is going bad . . . an article of clothing that is not in style anymore, that we do not want to wear again, goes to the poor."[3]

Mother Teresa pulled no punches. Remember, the Lord said, what we do for the least of our brothers and sisters we do for him. If Jesus were begging in front of you, what would you put in his bag?

He has given us a great responsibility to build heaven on earth. "The coming of the kingdom of God cannot be observed, and no one will announce, 'Look, here it is,' or, 'There it is.' For behold, the kingdom of God is among you" (Luke 17:20–21).

Like her Master, Mother Teresa was just as concerned about spiritual poverty as she was about economic deprivation. "Everybody today seems to be in a hurry," she proclaimed. "No one has any time to give to others; children to their parents, parents to their children, spouses to each other. World peace begins to break down in the homes." She noted this was especially true in developed, industrialized nations.[4]

We can be wealthy and yet lonely, poor in spirit, at war in the heart, suffering and forgotten, dying a cruel death inside.

And the humble Nobel Prize winner envisioned the end of life as our day in court. "At the moment of death we will not be judged according to the number of good deeds we have done or by the diplomas we have received in our lifetime," Mother Teresa predicted. "We will be judged according to the love we have put into our work."[5]

That makes perfect sense, because, according to the apostle John, God is love (see 1 John 4:8).

Someday time is going to run out on your life and mine, and God is going to weigh our mercy against our evil, our loving-kindness versus our selfishness, smugness, and lack of concern.

Love itself will measure the fullness of our compassion.

Jesus has already died to save us from sin. The question is: How well did we love him back? How grateful were we? What did we do to show gratitude?

St. Gregory of Nazianzus had some startling things to say on the importance of mercy versus sin. Gregory's father was a bishop, and Gregory reluctantly became a priest. He was destined to serve as a bishop himself and became a vital, outspoken leader during a very turbulent time in the early church. Today he is considered a Church Father and is acclaimed as "the Theologian."

Gregory, too, saw no loopholes in Matthew 25 and Jesus' command that we be merciful to those on the lower rungs of the social ladder. His take? Neglecting the poor is the ultimate insult to the one who was rich but became poor to save us.

"Do you think that compassion is not an obligation upon you but a matter of choice? Not rule but recommendation?" asked St. Gregory. "This is what I myself also should very much like to think, but I stand in terror of his left hand, and the goats, and the rebukes leveled against them by the one who has summoned them. They are condemned to take their places on the left not because they stole, or committed sacrilege, or fornicated or violated other taboo, but because they did not serve Christ through the poor."[6]

Does it surprise you that a bishop and saint would say it's not so much stealing or our lust that will damn us, but our self-centered, prideful lives that lack mercy?

Don't be confused. Following Jesus is all about obeying the law of love—all of it, in everything we do. Loving God and loving our neighbor. In that same homily, St. Gregory went on to encourage his flock to love the poor—like their lives depended on it.

> If, then, you place any credence in what I say, servants of Christ and brothers and fellow heirs, while we may, let us visit Christ, let us heal Christ, let us feed Christ, let us clothe Christ, let us welcome Christ, let us honor Christ, not with food alone like some; nor with ointments, like Mary; nor with tomb alone like, Joseph of Arimathea; nor with obsequies, like Nicodemus, who loved Christ in a half measure; nor with gold and frankincense and myrrh as the Magi did before these others. Rather, since the Lord of all will have *mercy, and not sacrifice*, and since a kind heart is worth more than myriads *of fat sheep*, this let us offer to him through the poor who are today downtrodden, so that when we depart this world they may receive us into the eternal habitations in Christ himself, our Lord, to whom be the glory forever. Amen.[7]

Sheep or goats? To which flock do you belong?

There is still time to produce some good, thick wool for the judgment scales.

FOUR

I Do What I Hate

It's never too late to change direction. No matter how far we've strayed from the Good Shepherd, he's ready to welcome us with open arms and carry us home on his shoulders.

Here's proof. In a parable, Jesus compares the kingdom of heaven to a landowner who hired day laborers to cultivate his vineyard. The employer began recruiting workers in the marketplace at dawn. They agreed to toil for the usual wage. Then the proprietor went in search of more willing workers at 9:00 a.m., noon, 3:00 p.m., and as late as 5:00 p.m. At each time, the boss offered the same day's wage.

As the sun dipped on the horizon, the vineyard owner sent out his foreman to gather the laborers to receive their earnings. He paid the 5:00 p.m. crew first, and as promised they got the full day's wage, even though they had worked just one hour. Now this excited those who had been hired first. They assumed they would get an even greater reward because they had been on the clock since morning. But they got the same amount. Nothing extra.

The early risers grumbled. They had suffered through the hottest hours of the day, yet they didn't earn a shekel more than those who barely broke a sweat in the late afternoon.

The landlord responded to one disgruntled laborer, "My friend, I am not cheating you. Did you not agree with me for the usual daily wage? Take what is yours and go. What if I wish to give this last one the same as you? [Or] am I not free to do as I wish with my own money? Are you envious because I am generous?" (Matthew 20:13–15). Jesus went on to explain, "Thus, the last will be first, and the first will be last" (v. 16).

Throughout Church history, there are many examples of late-comers—legendary sinners who transformed their lives to become hall of fame saints, not the least of whom is St. Augustine of Hippo. He was such a party animal and so strongly resisted Christianity that his mother, Monica, vaulted herself to sainthood by tearfully praying for his conversion. She was both charitable to those in need and profoundly patient and dedicated to her son's salvation. Although Augustine long delayed his baptism and acceptance of Jesus, he became one of the Church's great theological minds. Finally, Monica's son converted to Catholicism and became a doctor of the faith.

Now, before you put your feet up and figure you can procrastinate about your Christian conversion experience or rely on your grandmother's novenas, consider this. No one knows what time the sun will set on his or her life; we may be unavailable to labor in the Lord's vineyard in the late afternoon. Even with daylight savings time, the clouds might eclipse the sun as our golden hour fades to black. Death shows up without invitation and without regard for either the clock or the calendar.

Perhaps you're thinking, *It's hopeless. I've got too much garbage and too many skeletons in my closet to clean up. I'm a creature of habit. I've been hanging out with scraggly goats for too long. I'm addicted to sin.*

Well, here's your answer from a lifelong buddy of mine, a priest,

Father Joseph Marquis. He says, "Christianity is a twelve-step program for recovering sinners."

A twelve-step program?

You might be somewhat familiar with the twelve steps, developed by "Bill W.," co-founder of Alcoholics Anonymous (AA). These steps are now the basis of many other formal efforts to battle addiction, from overeating and gambling to narcotics and nicotine.

Most people who regularly attend twelve-step program support group meetings quickly make a profound discovery. *Everyone* could benefit from working the twelve steps, one day at a time. Even if you're not a fat guy, casino junkie, alcoholic, or smoker.

We're all addicted to something, someone, or someplace.

Unfortunately, if everyone showed up at AA or Overeaters Anonymous, there wouldn't be enough chairs at the support group tables or enough coffee to drink for the people recovering from alcoholism or gluttony.

Why does Fr. Joe compare Christianity to the twelve steps? Because the AA program is firmly based on building a relationship with God—with a higher power. "Bill W." was an incurable alcoholic before he had a transformational spiritual awakening and co-founded AA with "Dr. Bob," another desperate drinker.

The program's essential elements are admitting your powerlessness and turning your will and your life over to God. Those who successfully work the AA plan do more than become sober. They achieve serenity on a day-by-day basis by applying the principles of the twelve steps to every aspect of their lives.

Step One of Alcoholics Anonymous is: "We admitted we were powerless over *alcohol*—that our lives had become unmanageable."[8]

For Overeaters Anonymous it's: "We admitted we were power-less over *food*—that our lives had become unmanageable."[9]

You get the idea. Drugs. Smoking. Emotions. Clutter. Plug in your addiction and work the steps, one by one, until you reach step twelve—and then start all over again. You never graduate from the program.

As addicts experience spiritual growth, many develop remark-able wisdom. Some choose to replace the key word in the first step and swap it for a universal phrase that applies to all of us.

It then reads: "We admitted we were powerless over *people, places, and things*—that our lives had become unmanageable."

People, places, and things—that just about covers the universe.

Who or what are you addicted to?

Who or what are you trying to control?

Has your desire to manage others made your life chaotic?

Are you playing God by running other people's lives, trying to get the world and every event to fit into your earthly vision? If only everyone would just listen to you, right?

Meanwhile, how's *your* self-improvement going? Isn't it easier to fix someone else's life than it is to do the tough work of changing yourself?

Believe it or not, there's even a twelve-step group for people addicted to controlling people. It's called "Co-Dependents Anony-mous." I'll bet you know someone who qualifies for that program. Are you looking at your reflection again?

Jesus advises, "Stop judging, that you may not be judged" (Mat-thew 7:1).

This is the measure-twice-cut-once rule from our beloved

carpenter. Instead of wandering through life sweeping up the messy sawdust and splinters that other people create and then weighing them—the Lord recommends that we saw away the planks and boards obstructing the view of our own hearts and behavior.

Here's a challenge: See if you can make it through just one day without judging anyone. Unspoken criticism is also off limits. Try it sometime. Then try making it a habit.

Jesus speaks bluntly. He calls me a "hypocrite" for judging others without first correcting my own character defects (see Matthew 7:5). How can I have any credibility if I'm guilty of the same issue, perhaps displayed in a different manner? Maybe I don't pick up a bottle or gamble away my paycheck, but perhaps I can't set aside my job and my love of money or I jeopardize my marriage with risky, abusive behavior. Or I might not be an overeater, but I'm a world-class gossip—I can't stop talking about the flaws of others the way some people overindulge on French fries, chocolate, or potato chips.

"To be aware of a single shortcoming within oneself is more useful than to be aware of a thousand in somebody else." That piece of wisdom comes courtesy of the Dalai Lama.[10] I'm sure Jesus agrees. What value is there in cataloguing the faults of others? You can't change them. We can only hope to change ourselves for the better. And if we accomplish that, we can become good examples and cause others to say, "I want what she's got!"

This is an underlying theme of the "Serenity Prayer," which AA has helped to make so well known and beloved:

> God grant me the serenity
> to accept the things I cannot change;

the courage to change the things I can;
and the wisdom to know the difference.

Acceptance, courage, and wisdom.

In twelve-step programs, many recovering addicts come to understand and admit that their problem is much more than substance abuse or overindulgences. For most of us, our affliction is really self-centered fear. It's the desire to feel in control of everything and everybody. To play god. We're all guilty of it when we fail to trust our heavenly Father. The more fearful we are, the deeper our addictions can become because we feel comfortable, safely wrapped in their very familiar clutches, instead of the Lord's embrace.

These addictions help us deny reality and avoid the truth about life.

For example, so many of us deny the inevitability and unpredictability of death. And we irrationally fear our demise. We pretend we're going to live forever in this world.

What are we *most* afraid of?

An early departure? The death of children or grandchildren?

Saying good-bye to Mom and Dad?

Missing our family and friends? Feeling unloved?

Enduring a painful and nasty disease? Falling apart? Suicide?

The loneliness of death?

Declining status? Loss of our youth?

The end of our freedom and independence?

Fading vitality? Becoming unimportant? Forgotten?

Being betrayed by your body?

Growing fat or scrawny, old and wrinkled?

Suffering and weakness?

Losing your mind to senility or dementia?

Shrinking income and wealth? Poverty?

Anonymity? Embarrassment in our decline?

Dying unceremoniously? With all our regrets and fractured relationships?

The uncertainty of the afterlife?

Any and all of those thoughts are understandable. But our anxiety about misery and the end of life won't prevent them. On the other hand, ignoring our mortality doesn't make us immortal.

And our addiction to drama and self-pity won't buy us more time or more control.

Be honest. On a day-to-day basis, how many matters are really life-and-death? So why do we sweat the small stuff? Complain constantly? Why do so many of us behave like it's the end of the world when things don't go our way?

In *The Confessions,* St. Augustine observed that, remarkably, our selfish human instincts and fears begin with our first breaths. He noticed the "me-me" behavior in infants and toddlers.

Who can recall to me the sins I committed as a baby? It can hardly be right for a child, even at that age, to cry for everything, including things which would harm him; to work himself into a tantrum against people older than himself and not required to obey him; and to try his best to strike and hurt others who know better than he does, including his own parents, when they do not give in to him and refuse to pander to his whims which would only do him harm.[11]

Does that sound like any teens or adults you know? If you look in the mirror, do you resemble those remarks in any way? Keep in mind, few are "required to obey" us. Do you ever behave like a spoiled brat to manipulate others so they do what you want?

"This shows that, if babies are innocent, it is not for lack of will to do harm, but for lack of strength," Augustine concluded.[12] He's right. We are willful and selfish and often do destructive things to force others into submission. This ultimately hurts God, our families, our friends—and ourselves.

Our Lord is asking us for the opposite—to accept his will. To have the courage to throw ourselves into his arms, trusting him completely with our lives and our deaths, while becoming selfless and merciful in order to love and serve him.

No fear. Now, that's wisdom.

That's why AA Step Three is: "Made a decision to turn our will and lives over to the care of God *as we understood him*."[13]

What is your understanding of God?

What kind of relationship do you have with him?

How much do you love him? More than the people in your family?

What are you doing to get to know God and understand him better?

What have you done to let go and let God catch you?

Perhaps you're in denial. You think, *I'm not an addict*. The late, esteemed psychiatrist and author, Gerald G. May, MD, lists more than 150 addictions of attraction and aversion in his book, *Addiction & Grace: Love and Spirituality in the Healing of Addiction*. These include behaviors like envy, gossiping, nail biting, and being right, as well as our over-commitment to fishing, family, friends, money, politics, and death. Almost anything can be pursued in excess, except genuine, unconditional love.[14]

This psychiatrist and spiritual counselor is widely recognized for contributions he made to psychology by connecting our unquenchable desire for God with a scientific understanding of our behaviors. In the first chapter of *Addiction & Grace*, Dr. May concurs with the diagnosis offered by St. Paul: We long for love and all God's grace, but we are addicted to sin. We stuff ourselves full of worldly things to fill the hole in our hearts, but that doesn't satisfy the hunger for the divine.

"What I do, I do not understand. For I do not do what I want, but I do what I hate," St. Paul wrote in Romans 7:15. And he's a saint! But like all sinners, every saint has a past.

Evil deadens our senses and leaves our minds calloused and unaware of the God-given craving to feel his love and love him back. To personally know the one who made us. The one who counts the very hairs on our heads (see Luke 12:7).

Like kids stuffing their faces at the cookie jar, we too often choose temporary pleasures that eventually make us sick, rather than choosing what we know is good, that which makes us healthy and happy.

The master carpenter has the perfect plan for our reconstruction. Chop and chisel away at the idols in our lives, the selfish sin that is cluttering our own vision and perspective, until we begin to clearly see the world—finding Jesus in everyone we meet and humbly serving God with all we do.

You might be surprised to learn that twelve-step programs for anonymous alcoholics, overeaters, gamblers, and co-dependents are in lockstep with the Lord's "judge not" gospel. The emphasis is removing the planks and timbers from our eyes before we even think about reaching for the specks of wood in our brothers' and sisters' eyes.

In fact, recovering addicts support each other at meetings by sharing their "experience, strength, and hope" and by being there to "just listen" to their friends in the program. They rarely offer advice unless asked or are fulfilling the role of an addict's "sponsor"—a trusted, chosen advisor and twelve-step veteran.

Consider traveling life's road by following the Gospels along with this spiritual tool: an adapted version of the twelve steps of AA. I expanded on the language to cover every one of us in recovery, regardless of our addictions. Recommended speed: one day at a time.

1. "We admitted we were powerless over *people, places, and things*—that our lives had become unmanageable." *(Who or what am I addicted to? I will stop my denial. I don't have to lie to myself anymore.)*

2. "We came to believe that a Power greater than ourselves could restore us to sanity." *(Sin is crazy. One definition of insanity is doing the same thing again and again, and expecting different results. Why do I continue to hurt God, others, and myself, often in the same ways?)*

3. "We made a decision to turn our will and our lives over to the care of God *as we understood him.*" *("Thy kingdom come, thy will be done on earth as it is in heaven." If God is my co-pilot, I'm sitting in the wrong seat. I need his hands on the controls. I'm going where he takes me.)*

4. "We made a searching and fearless moral inventory of ourselves." *(That's an inventory of both good and bad characteristics. Note to self: This is my moral inventory, not my neighbor's.)*

5. "We admitted to God, to ourselves, and to another human being the exact nature of our wrongs." *(Sounds a lot like confession, doesn't it? That's a good way for Catholics to fulfill this step.)*

6. "We were entirely ready to have God remove all these defects of character." *(Am I really ready to change for the better? Have I thoroughly examined my conscience? Am I prepared to do the heavy lifting? Am I ready to grow spiritually?)*

7. "We humbly asked him to remove our shortcomings." *(Here's where I hit my knees and tell God I'm convinced I can't change without his help. I need divine healing.)*

8. "We made a list of all the persons we had harmed, and became willing to make amends to them all." *(Do I realize how many people I've hurt? And that includes sticking my nose into their business without an invitation to do so. Or the opposite: ignoring someone who has asked me for support, even a stranger.)*

9. "We made direct amends to such people wherever possible, except when to do so would injure them or others." *(I will develop the humility and courage to be able to say, "I'm sorry" and then prove it by my behavior.)*

10. "We continued to take personal inventory and when we were wrong promptly admitted it." *(Progress not perfection . . . hour by hour . . . day by day . . . I will strive to be a saint, a sinner in recovery.)*

11. "We sought through prayer and meditation to improve our conscious contact with God *as we understood him,* praying only for knowledge of his will for us and the power to carry that out." *(Shaking my addiction to sin depends on my relationship with God. The more I rely on him, the better. "Let go and let God" is a vital AA slogan.)*

12. "Having had a spiritual awakening as the result of these steps, we tried to carry this message *to those like us, who are addicted to sin,* and to practice these principles in all our affairs." *(Being unselfish, sharing love, understanding, service, and mercy with everyone I meet is the key to living in serenity. That's heaven on earth.)*[15]

Of course, Jesus managed to say all this much more simply:

"You shall love the Lord, your God, with all your heart, with all your soul, and with all your mind. This is the greatest and the first commandment. The second is like it: You shall love your neighbor as yourself. The whole law and the prophets depend on these two commandments." (Matthew 22:37–40)

Thousands of pages of the Bible boiled down to fifty-one words. The Ten Commandments and more than six hundred Old Testament laws became just two.

No confusion.

No fine print.

No loopholes.

God yearns for our love. All of it. He wants us to swap our addictions to this world for a sublime love for him and heaven. And only in that way do we escape death and live forever.

St. Paul put it this way:

> But thanks be to God that, although you were once slaves of sin, you have become obedient from the heart to the pattern of teaching to which you were entrusted. Freed from sin, you have become slaves of righteousness. For the wages of sin is death, but the gift of God is eternal life in Christ Jesus our Lord. (Romans 6:17–18, 23)

It's not too late to join the crew that's laboring in the vineyard and earn our heavenly wage. But we can't put it off. The sun is always setting somewhere, on someone.

And if you need help changing for the better, talk to a priest. Remember, Christianity is a twelve-step program for recovering sinners like you and me.

FIVE

Drinking Poison

"You have to be ready," the nurse said to my wife, Ellen. She was talking about preparing to die.

Her name was Analyn. This Filipina Catholic had spent much of her career caring for seriously ill people.

As I sat in Ellen's hospital room the day after her six-hour surgery, Analyn shared stories about her experiences with breast cancer patients. She talked about serving so many women who despair and become seriously depressed after doctors amputate their breasts.

Analyn opened up while she tenderly and vigilantly attended to Ellen's needs. Her work is a constant reminder of death. With the explosion of pink ribbons, burly pro athletes wearing pink, and the staggering number of women suffering breast cancer, it should be much harder for all of us to forget our mortality for too long.

This exceptional nurse was not warning my wife to anticipate the end because of unstable vital signs or an ominous pathology report. She was actually complimenting Ellen on her positive, grateful attitude post-surgery. Analyn had learned the best way to live is day by day, fully appreciating each moment and each person, while always being totally prepared to die.

"Be ready."

That's uncommon advice from a healthcare professional. She

offered no recommendation on a fountain of youth prescription to avoid the inevitable. In her own gentle way, Analyn was reminding us that even if Ellen achieves lasting remission, which is very likely, eventually death will come calling anyway—for each of us.

Coincidentally, just the day before, during Ellen's surgical ordeal, I sat in the waiting room with a geneticist, our dear friend Sue Caumartin Stewart. She was reading the best seller, *Being Mortal*, by Atul Gawande, MD, MPH. This gifted surgeon reveals medicine's challenge to communicate the truth to dying patients. He candidly discusses the way physicians sometimes overpromise the positive outcomes of debilitating therapies for patients with long odds for survival. For example, chemo for those who have months or weeks to live actually drains many lives. Too many patients spend their final days and hours suffering, exhausted, and continuously sleeping after stressful, grueling interventions. They have little energy left to share with loved ones.

Some doctors feel obliged to stretch the promises of medical facts in order to give families hope—because many medical professionals are ill-equipped to treat the end of life.

Gawande explains that doctors fix people and illnesses, but two things are beyond repair: aging and death.[16]

Christians know the only fix for those conditions is Jesus.

"I am the resurrection and the life; whoever believes in me, even if he dies, will live, and everyone who lives and believes in me will never die" (John 11:25–26). That's what the Lord told Martha. He asked her if she believed him, while her brother Lazarus lay in his tomb. Lazarus had passed away four days earlier. Yet Martha had faith in Jesus as the Messiah, the Son of God. So did her sister, Mary.

And Jesus wept for his dead friend moments before he raised him up! Lazarus lived again.

Do *you* believe it?

What's the best way to demonstrate that we are convinced of the resurrection and the life?

How do we get ready to die and live forever?

Here's a good approach. I once met a man I'll call "Steve." He was old, a widower, and he could hear death knocking. So he started to let go of this world. He lived in a simple, very comfortable home and was a devout Catholic. Steve had all the basic things he required, but he knew the same wasn't true for many in his community.

He began to donate hundreds of dollars each month to help the needy in our neighborhood. Sometimes his monthly charitable gift was a thousand dollars. Sometimes it was two thousand.

When asked why he was making the sizeable regular donations, Steve said, "I don't want to die with the money." In fact, he insisted the cash be used to help the poor buy extra food.

"Like steak," Steve specified.

Obviously, he had read Matthew 25 or had heard the teaching, "Whatever you do for the least of my brothers, you do for me."

Steve wasn't going to feed Jesus with a can of soup, a generic box of cereal, a tuna sandwich, a hot dog, or even a burger. He was buying steaks for strangers, and he did it very quietly. Few people at the church knew. His practice continued for years until one day he had run out of spare funds.

Now Steve was ready. A year or so later he died. Can you imagine what he must have felt as he breathed his last? He believed in the promise of the resurrection. He had children and grandchildren, but

Steve had chosen to give away some of his estate while he was still alive.

We can all be inspired that Steve had thrown a monthly feast for the lame, the poor, the lonely, the forgotten, the sick, the deprived—people he didn't know at all.

Can you picture the faces of those needy people when they purchased delicious food they otherwise couldn't afford? How do you think that made them feel about their lives? About people in their community? About God and his mercy?

They probably felt loved, even if for just that brief moment.

I imagine Steve thought about that often as he grew older and knew his days were numbered.

Now, what was our Lord thinking as he approached his last day of human life? How did he prepare for his death?

Facing crucifixion, Jesus Christ did everything he asks of us in our daily lives. He walked the talk and then some.

For example, at the Last Supper, just hours before Judas betrayed him and Jesus was arrested, the Lord humbled himself before his disciples. He washed their feet. Remember, it was St. John the Baptist, Jesus' cousin, who said he was unworthy to even loosen the Messiah's sandal strap (see John 1:27). Yet the Son of God set the ultimate example and served those he had taught. He even washed the feet of Judas, his betrayer.

Jesus said he did these things to model behavior for his disciples. Not just those who shared his last Passover meal, but those of us who gather around his Eucharistic table today.

Have I washed any feet lately?

Do I need to humble myself and serve anyone?

In the Garden of Gethsemane, after Judas betrayed Jesus with a kiss, a fight broke out. Peter severed the ear of the high priest's slave. Yet Jesus halted the melee and healed the man's wound, making him whole again.

Do I care about the health of those who have injured me?

Do I pray for my enemies? Do I rejoice in their blessings?

From the cross, Jesus prayed to his heavenly Father, "Forgive them, they know not what they do" (Luke 23:34). Nailed to the tree, somehow his laboring heart was filled with mercy for those who unjustly accused and crucified him.

Am I harboring any resentment?

Many spiritual writers have shared a variation of this adage: "Holding a grudge is like drinking poison and waiting for your adversary to die." It only makes us sick.

Likewise, it's no accident that when the disciples asked Jesus to "teach us to pray," he responded with the simple genius of the Our Father, which includes: "Forgive us our trespasses as we forgive those who trespass against us." This is a petition we should not offer casually or by rote. It requires serious, heartfelt consciousness. We're actually asking God to forgive us in the same manner that we forgive others. I once heard a priest say the Lord's Prayer was the most dangerous appeal, because every time we say it, we're imploring God to weigh our mercy toward others—and measure an equal portion of compassion for us when he renders his judgment of our offenses.

And the author of that prayer lives up to his word, even as he was enduring an unjust execution, amidst ridicule and insult. Remember the ornery criminal hanging on a cross next to Jesus? He jeered, "Are you not the Messiah? Save yourself and us" (Luke 23:39).

What happened next? Did the Lord condemn him? Not at all. He "turned the other cheek" and said nothing. And when the other crucified thief defended the Lord and asked for his compassion, Jesus replied, "Amen, I say to you, today you will be with me in Paradise" (Luke 23:43).

Jesus demonstrated unwavering forgiveness of the guilty—with arms wide open to welcome the repentant sinner.

Am I seeking revenge on anyone in my heart? Can I let that go and be merciful?

Jesus not only forgave Peter for denying him three times, he made him the leader of his Church. Now that's forgiving *and* forgetting.

Remember, Jesus had told Peter to forgive a repeat offender seventy-seven times (see Matthew 18:22).

Is there someone I love who has deeply hurt me? Can I be happy without forgiving her?

From the cross, Jesus made sure his aging, widowed mother would be safe after his death. He assigned the apostle John to care for her, and Mary would now parent young John, the beloved disciple. All this, just before the Lord used his dying breath to commend his soul to his Father. That's unselfish love.

Is there someone who needs my tender care and concern?

Am I committing my love each day to God? Do I truly worship and trust him, or am I just going to church on Sunday because it's tradition?

Service. Forgiveness. Compassion. Love and mercy. Trusting God's will. Jesus demonstrated all these behaviors right to the bitter end. He showed us how love conquers death to roll away the stone and win the resurrection and the life.

This is why St. John Paul II proclaimed, "Do not abandon

yourselves to despair. We are the Easter people, and hallelujah is our song."[17]

I'm confident he would have agreed with Nurse Analyn when she told her cancer patient, "Be ready."

Be ready—just like Jesus and Steve were.

Do you believe in the resurrection like Martha and Mary did?

Are you prepared for your Easter? Are you ready to conquer death and live forever?

SIX

Lady Poverty

"Good teacher, what must I do to inherit eternal life?" (Mark 10:17). The rich young man who raised that question would soon be sorry he asked. But not initially. First the Lord told him to obey the Ten Commandments. When the wealthy guy responded that he had faithfully followed them since he was a kid, Jesus upped the ante. He looked at the affluent believer and appreciated his sincerity.

Feeling love for him, the Lord threw the man a lifeline of truth: "You are lacking in one thing. Go, sell what you have, and give to [the] poor and you will have treasure in heaven; then come, follow me" (Mark 10:21).

Pow! Right in the wallet. Oh, that hurt! The man was crestfallen. He was loaded and owned a lot of property. Sell it all? Give the proceeds to the poor? Was Jesus delusional? Who would do that?

One of the world's most beloved saints, St. Nicholas of Myra, was another rich kid. According to Church tradition, he inherited his parents' money after they died in an epidemic. St. Nick chose the priesthood over a fancy life and became a bishop at a young age, known for his charity. The "boy bishop," as some called him, gave away his wealth to people in need in his homeland of Asia Minor, modern-day Turkey.

Nicholas performed his acts of kindness in secret—just as Jesus tells us to keep our good deeds so humble and quiet that even our left hand doesn't know when, where, or how our right hand has lifted someone up.

That's why Santa Claus still arrives in the dark of night. The commercialized character is cast in the tradition of the hallowed bishop, who is "ho-ho-holy" and rich in heavenly treasure. Once well-off and comfortable, Nicholas' zeal for Christ bought him several years in prison under the Roman emperor, Diocletian, who persecuted Christians, martyring some. When Constantine took the Roman throne and became a Christian convert, St. Nicholas was freed. He returned to his ministry, even attending the Council of Nicaea. Bishop Nicholas traded his earthly inheritance for sainthood, and his concern for the poor earned him iconic status as the patron of children, young and old.[18]

As a boy, St. Francis of Assisi was spoiled by his parents. His father, Pietro di Bernadone, was a successful cloth merchant. Francis became a very popular young guy, good at business. He had fancy tastes with a penchant for spending, partying, and womanizing. After serving as a knight, enduring confinement as a prisoner of war, and suffering serious illness, Francis had a remarkable Christian conversion. It spurred him to walk away from his family's riches to follow Jesus and live in extreme austerity. Wearing nothing but rags, he actually left his disapproving father and his textile fortune, saying, "From now on I can say with complete freedom, 'Our Father who art in heaven.'"[19]

As the founder of the Franciscan Order of Friars Minor, St. Francis has millions of followers, friars, nuns, and lay apostles across the globe—not to mention many Franciscan saints who emulated this once rich young man. St. Francis said he gave up wealth to marry "Lady Poverty." This was a "metaphor for the paradoxes of the Gospel: richness in poverty, strength in our weakness," and the ability to find genuine, unconditional love by jilting the embrace of worldly things.[20]

St. Francis believed wealth was a prison and poverty was true liberty. "If we had any possessions we should need weapons and laws to defend them," he said.[21]

Incidentally, Francis offered this simple but undeniable reminder about death: "Remember that when you leave this earth, you can take with you nothing that (you) have received—only what you have given."[22]

Francis is also renowned for respecting all those he met, whether the pope, a leper, a beggar, or wild creatures while he chatted with them in God's creation. He believed that we belong to one family—our Creator's.

Catholics, Protestants, and even non-Christians love St. Francis of Assisi for the moving examples he set. In 2013, the newly elected pope, Cardinal Jorge Mario Bergoglio, surprised many by choosing the name "Francis" for his papacy. Although a Jesuit, the Holy Father's words and actions have cast a strong, Franciscan-shaped shadow, complete with hooded habit. He has focused on issues dear to the beloved saint from Assisi, shining a powerful light of truth and compassion on the needs of the poor and our planet.

Today, millions of gardens worldwide include a statue of this penniless Italian friar. How many people do you know who own sculptures of Bill Gates, Warren Buffet, Jim Walton, Donald Trump, Steve Jobs, or Thomas Edison? But I'll bet you've seen at least one St.

Francis of Assisi figurine in a place of respect. Jesus says, "For everyone who exalts himself will be humbled, but the one who humbles himself will be exalted" (Luke 14:11).

The prayer attributed to St. Francis is one of the world's most cherished prayers:

> Lord, make me an instrument of your peace . . . grant that I may not so much seek to be consoled as to console; to be understood as to understand; to be loved as to love; For it is in giving that we receive; it is in pardoning that we are pardoned; it is in dying that we are born again to eternal life.

There's an ongoing debate as to whether or not St. Francis of Assisi really said, "Preach the Gospel at all times. Use words if necessary." Maybe he didn't say it exactly that way; however, there is no doubt that he wrote this rule on preaching for his brother friars: "Let all the brothers preach by their works."

And this one on love:

> And let them show their love by the works they do for each other, according as the Apostle says: "Let us not love in word or in tongue, but in deed and in truth." Let them "speak evil of no man," nor murmur, nor detract others, for it is written: "Whisperers and detractors are hateful to God."
>
> Let them not judge and not condemn, and, as the Lord says, let them not pay attention to the least sins of others, but rather let them recount their own in the bitterness of their soul.[23]

Regarding the poor, he said: "It would be considered a theft on our part if we didn't give to someone in greater need than we are."[24]

Does that sound like anyone you know? When it comes to letting go of this world, St. Francis of Assisi was a radical like his master, Jesus. He was very serious about following Christ's gospel, and modeling the Messiah who was homeless and certainly no property owner. Jesus was born in a manger and buried in a donated tomb. "Foxes have dens and birds of the sky have nests, but the Son of Man has nowhere to rest his head," Jesus told a scribe who wanted to be his disciple (Matthew 8:20).

Likewise, Francis of Assisi embraced poverty. He abandoned the cushiness of the rich merchant class, shedding the luxurious fabrics of his father's textile sales business in exchange for a coarse tunic and Christlike simplicity and austerity. He preached to all, converting and captivating many, including storied conversations with the birds of the air and a ferocious wolf. He is said to have preached a homily on gratitude to his feathered friends. This behavior earned him the title "God's fool" as well as thousands of followers who were powerfully inspired by his simple, meaningful messages and dedication to actually practicing the revolutionary lifestyle the gospel preaches. It's a lifestyle that puts people, especially the marginalized, before wealth and power.

Among his lay disciples was Elizabeth of Hungary. At fourteen this young princess married Ludwig IV of Germany and they had three children together. While Elizabeth was still a teen, she also began following the teachings of Francis of Assisi. The young queen funded construction of a hospital for the poor in honor of St. Francis, and during a famine her charity fed nine hundred people daily. She worked in the community in simple clothing.

When Elizabeth was only twenty, Ludwig died. Members of the royal court mocked her for squandering her treasure on commoners. She persisted in service, sharing her wealth with the poor and homeless, visiting and caring for the patients in the hospital she had founded. Elizabeth became affiliated with the third order of St. Francis, never remarried, and died at age twenty-four, just five years after St. Francis of Assisi. She was canonized a saint shortly after her death.[25]

Why do we so admire people who reject this world to help the less fortunate?

Is it because we recognize goodness, and intuitively know the grace of God when we see it? St. Nicholas walked the earth more than sixteen hundred years ago. St. Francis has been dead nearly eight hundred years. Yet they are both widely revered in the impersonal, digital age of the twenty-first century, where both the virtual and the real worlds adore wealth so much that we've invented new ways to worship it.

But as the Bible says, greed has long been the root of *all* evil (see 1 Timothy 6:10). Jesus noted that it's harder for the wealthy to enter a heavenly mansion in his Father's kingdom than it is for a camel to slip through the narrow city gates. However, he added that all things are possible with God (see Mark 10:25–27).

Sts. Nicholas, Francis, and Elizabeth succeeded at shaking the burdens of affluence and following the Lord. But is it realistic to expect anyone to follow their lead today? Certainly their ancient times were different, right?

Indeed they were. There were no social safety nets like unemployment benefits, food stamps, Social Security, Medicaid, Medicare, or other public assistance. Their risk was greater than ours. Walking away from wealth likely made you a beggar or committed you to an austere monastery or convent.

Do you know anyone who would desert riches for rags to follow our Lord and Savior?

Meet Jason Brown, another rich young man who apparently lost his worldly mind. In 2012, at twenty-nine years old, he left pro football to become a farmer and give away his crops to the poor. According to Brown, his agent told him he was making the mistake of a lifetime.

Now before you surmise that Brown's career was all washed up, read his résumé. He was once considered among the very best centers in the National Football League. In fact, at one point, he signed a five-year, $37.5 million deal, making him the highest paid player at his position. Even when the St. Louis Rams eventually cut him, other teams stepped up to express interest in landing Brown, including the Baltimore Ravens.

Why did number sixty hang up his spikes? "Love is the most wonderful currency that you can give anyone," he told *CBS News* in 2014. He considers a life of service true success in God's eyes, and that year he reportedly raised and donated some 100,000 pounds of sweet potatoes and 10,000 pounds of cucumbers grown on his First Fruits Farm in North Carolina. All those veggies went to local food pantries to feed the needy. Brown's goal was to double that donation in 2015. By the way, he had never farmed before and learned to till and harvest from YouTube videos and his neighbors. As the owner of 1,000 acres, Brown had enormous capacity to redefine the miracle of the loaves and fishes.[26]

"Amen, amen, I say to you, whoever believes in me will do the works that I do, and will do greater ones than these, because I am going to the Father," Jesus said in John 14:12. Brown is living proof that all things are possible when working the Lord's plan. On the other hand, maybe the NFL's water boys are serving up holy water, because, although Brown is rare, he is not one-of-a-kind.

Eric Mahl was once a promising linebacker for the Cleveland Browns and then the New York Jets. In 2014 I met Mahl and heard him speak at Benedictine University while participating in a spiritual conference in suburban Chicago, Illinois. His personal story is riveting. Mahl embodied Jesus' instructions to the "rich young man" by shunning the wealth he'd earned on the gridiron along with the adulation of family and fans. Somehow he summoned immense courage and sold his possessions, gave the money to the poor, and even lived on the streets with the homeless in order to bring them the good news of Divine Mercy.

The Ohio native grew up in a Catholic family that never missed Mass on Sunday. Although he felt drawn to Jesus at a young age, in high school Mahl had an all-consuming passion for football that inspired him to earn a Division-I scholarship to Kent State University. He then defied even longer odds by making the NFL. He became quite a physical specimen with a reputation as a take-no-prisoners linebacker. Reportedly Mahl could bench press 450 pounds.

Yet all the while, he felt his heart muscle tugging him toward the Lord. At Benedictine University, Mahl told the college audience he lived a dual life, reading spiritual books and praying fervently while downplaying and even concealing his faith from his teammates.

The Holy Spirit continued to coach Mahl through his self-described addiction to the game and his desire to perform. In 2013, at thirty years old, Mahl told Trent Beattie in the *National Catholic Register*, "I was so heavily into football, but it wasn't for football's sake; it was for my own. So I'd say my idol was really myself. It wasn't so much the game of football itself that drew me, as it was the challenge of being the best at it. I would work out twice and sometimes even three times a day, just to ensure I would be the strongest player on the team."[27]

When he signed with Cleveland in 2005, Mahl began struggling with his newfound success. "I never felt comfortable with the extreme wealth and all the glitz of professional football," he confessed.[28]

That same year, the Browns waived him, and the New York Jets picked up his contract. Mahl was ready to turn his will and life over to Jesus. Recalling this pivotal time in his life, he told the students at the Benedictine University conference that he was secretly attending Mass every day before practice, sincerely praying the Jets would cut him from their roster. And then it happened. "Eric, you're the hardest working guy on this team, but we have to let you go," management told him.

Although he cried about the end of his football career, he soon felt tremendous relief and began a spiritual pilgrimage to find his new vocation. After taking some time for discernment while successfully working in medical equipment sales, Mahl sold his home and gave away his possessions—except what he was wearing and one spare change of clothes. Donating his wealth to the needy, Mahl informed his family that he intended to become a hermit.

"Many people thought I was depressed, but they didn't know I was in love. I was in love with God, and I wanted to spend the rest of my life in prayer and sacrifice, alone with him," Mahl told the *Register*.[29]

To prepare himself for God's team, the former NFL player moved to Texas to live in a community of Carmelite hermits. Intense prayer, meditation, and reading the Gospel flipped Mahl's perspective of mankind. "I could then see that God was asking me to love him in the poor and rejected."[30]

After three years in a hermitage, Mahl began a spiritual odyssey that included a visit to the National Shrine of Divine Mercy in Stockbridge, Massachusetts. There he met Fr. Michael Gaitley, MIC, director of the Association of Marian Helpers. Fr. Gaitley encouraged Mahl to "be Divine Mercy" to others.

This once rich young man embraced that challenge and headed home to minister to Cleveland's less fortunate. And just as he had done with football, he poured his whole heart into his new vocation. Living among the street people and sleeping in shelters, Mahl engaged the suffering poor on a very personal level and shared the Lord's love for them. However, his words of Divine Mercy were not always welcome.

"I was also rejected by some people in the Church," Mahl explained. "Some people at a certain parish thought highly of a pro football player in 2005, but judgmentally of a homeless man in 2012."[31]

A year later, Mahl returned to Stockbridge, where he now lives at the National Shrine for the Divine Mercy as a layman. His mission is to assist the Marian Helpers in their outreach to the marginalized.

Reflecting on his year with the homeless, Mahl discovered an ironic truth. "It might sound depressing, but it was actually the most hope-filled time of my life," he shared.

"I look back now and see how merciful God has been in my life," he explained. "It's beautiful how he took my self-centered desire for greatness and transformed it into a desire to do all things for the greater glory of God and the salvation of all souls.

"Jesus' commandment to love our neighbor as he loves us is radical. To love one's enemies is radical, and to be merciful as he is merciful is radical," Mahl added.

"In the United States, there are many places for the poor to get food, clothing and shelter," Mahl said. "However, what is far, far more difficult to get is another person's time. People often don't want to take the time to listen to the poor, to interact with them as fellow human beings . . . living as a homeless man, there were no boundaries for me to be their brother. I was able to give them what is so often lacking."[32]

In the context of life and death, time is our greatest earthly possession. As the saying goes, "they're not making any more of it." Time is the only non-renewable resource. Once spent, you can't get it back. It's precious, especially for busy, successful people. Most of us will donate some money to a good cause, but it's hard to find truly committed volunteers.

Even if we're not materially rich, the conveniences of modern life and technology save most of us enormous amounts of time.

Do we use that time to make more money and have more fun or to serve others?

Are we willing to share our time with God? With those in need?

How much of your time would you give to help the poor?

Have you ever spoken to a poor person on the street? Visited a poor family in their home?

When it comes to your faith, how radical are you?

How much do you really love the Lord? Will you look for him in others, even the marginalized?

What aspect of your worldly life are you willing to give up for him—just a little?

Could you sacrifice some binge viewing of sports or TV shows? A portion of your fashionable wardrobe? A few of your favorite delicacies? Some of the time you dedicate to pursue awards and prestige in your profession? A bit of your bonus? Facebook, Instagram, Pinterest, and Twitter time? A fraction of your golfing, bowling, or fishing hobby?

Do you think you'd be happier if you focused less on yourself and more on God and others?

How far would you go to be spiritually happy?

Could you be the next St. Nicholas?

Or a modern St. Francis?

Are you perhaps more like St. Elizabeth of Hungary?

Could you do what Jason Brown or Eric Mahl did?

What will you do to inherit eternal life? The "rich young man" was hoping he could earn it without sacrificing too much.

Will we die like the Pharaohs of ancient Egypt, and delude ourselves into believing we can take our possessions with us? Ironically, the back of a U.S. dollar bill features a pyramid right next to the words: IN GOD WE TRUST.

Will you follow in the path of Jesus, or walk like an Egyptian?

It's time to decide.

SEVEN

Let's Be Frank

Before you die, do you think the world will see another Mother Teresa?

Could it be anyone you know? Will it be you? Why not? You'd be amazed what you can accomplish with God, if you're willing to do more than give lip service to your faith.

Here's what can happen if you just get started and give the Lord a little of your time.

Some people call Freddie Power of North Carolina a "modern-day Mother Teresa." This energetic and faith-filled grandmother is serving hundreds of the homeless on the streets of Charlotte. In 2008 Power felt the call to empty her bank account, buy food, and minister to a growing homeless community. She began by feeding people from her car. In a video at her website, this sidewalk evangelist reported that twenty people she served that first day turned their lives over to Jesus.

She said God told her to go back to the same neighborhood the following weekend. Again people came and she provided more food, shared the gospel, and prayed with them. She noted that twenty folks committed their lives to God that second week, too.

Power said the Lord told her to bring chairs the next time. So, with just three plastic chairs, she started the first of two missions on the streets and parking lots of Charlotte, where Power continues to nourish the homeless and the hungry with bread baked on earth and seasoned with heaven.

"When God comes and changes somebody, you don't do anything but show up and love them," she said. "Just show up and love them, and put your arms around them and hug them when they're crying, and they're transformed. Their lives are transformed."[33]

Power has come away from her experiences with compelling insights regarding those who Jesus speaks of in "The Sheep and the Goats Clause"—the hungry; the lonely; the unwelcome stranger; those who wear tattered clothing; the addicted; the sick and dying; the prisoner; the forgotten.

"We never tell them they need to be on a ten-step program or anything; we just love them and take their hands and pray for them. And now they're getting jobs and their lives are changing," she added.[34]

Power's website reports that her ministry has grown to serve international missions in the Dominican Republic, Africa, and Central America. Whether you picture her at work in the sketchy neighborhoods of Charlotte or in a village in Mozambique, when she speaks about the broken and the deprived, her words sound a lot like Blessed Mother Teresa's. "God loves them. He loves them, he loves them, he loves them. He outrageously loves the poor," Power said.[35]

She's not pretending to be the little nun in the striped Indian sari. In fact, Power is a tall, blonde, attractive evangelical Christian. But watching her in action enhances the resemblance to the Catholic founder of the Missionaries of Charity. The Christian Broadcasting Network captured Power and some of her homeless friends in a July

2013 video report.[36] It reveals that this devout Christian laywoman knows her neighbors well and is part of the lives of those she feeds, just as Mother Teresa personally embraced the destitute she served for decades.

You can see Jesus in both women.

Wouldn't you like to meet Freddie Power, Eric Mahl, and Jason Brown? Do they seem real to you, or are they a little bit like spiritual superheroes? Do you know anyone as dedicated to the gospel as they are? Could you spend a day each month doing what they do full time?

These three individuals are all living in the same twenty-first century world we experience. Yet they are among a spiritually enthralled minority who appear to be saints in the "hood." Aggressively pursuing heaven, they are walking among us in the footsteps of Christ. They're dying to this world. Abandoning conventional social practices in radical ways has left them seemingly happy and prepared to die—joyful and at peace.

How does someone find the courage to turn away from our modern herd mentality and shepherd the Lord's flock of lonely and forgotten? How does someone find the time and resources to tend the marginalized and lost sheep?

Maybe you've got kids and can't picture yourself taking the risk of mingling with the deprived, especially on America's mean streets. Many of the homeless are mentally ill or addicted and frightening, right?

Or perhaps you're older with physical challenges and can't imagine how you'd find enough energy. Or you might be younger, burning both ends of the candle, chasing your future with no time to share, even with those you love dearly.

The call to evangelize can seem overwhelming. But as we've seen, it begins with a single, brave step to actually walk the talk of the Gospel—and love Jesus by our actions—not just our words.

As Christians, anything less is hypocrisy.

It was *that* accusation that inspired college student, Frederic Ozanam, to found the Society of St. Vincent de Paul. In 1831, the eighteen-year-old arrived at the University of Paris, the School of Law at the Sorbonne. He enjoyed participating in a discussion club he had organized with Emmanuel Bailly, editor of the newspaper, *Tribune Catholique*. During lectures, when some professors would scoff at Christianity, young Ozanam would leap to defend the teachings of his faith. He and Bailly formed the student organization "Conference of History" to wax eloquently with students interested in serious academic topics. Ozanam seized the opportunity to cultivate a small group of likeminded Catholic apologists, shielding the Church from criticism and fulfilling "his vow of truth" to the faith he loved.

But talk is cheap and a vulnerable defense against moral critics.

One day, he faced an exceptionally uncomfortable and personal question. Ozanam was debating current events with other students, including agnostics and atheists in his club. He highlighted the role of Christianity in civilization, and one of his opponents acknowledged the good the Church had done in the past. But then his challenger's rebuttal stabbed Frederic between the ribs: "Let us be frank, Mr. Ozanam; let us also be very particular. What do you do besides talk to prove the faith you claim is in you?" asked his adversary.[37]

Perhaps the debater was only mouthing the words that the Lord was speaking through him. They proved to transfigure the young law student. Later, one of Ozanam's companions suggested they form a separate organization of Christian brothers to live out their faith in actions to benefit the needy.

Not long after, Ozanam provided the leadership that would help establish an inspired grassroots Christian outreach, comprised primarily of lay men and women.

The Society of St. Vincent de Paul was born on April 23, 1833, Ozanam's twentieth birthday, when he met with his pal Bailly and five other students to form an association of goodwill that would help them serve "the poor, needy and suffering."[38]

With guidance from Sister Rosalie Rendu, a Daughter of Charity, Ozanam and his co-founders began calling on the much less fortunate in the tenements of Paris. These Vincentians traveled in pairs to visit their needy clients, just as Jesus had commissioned his disciples.[39] "For where two or three are gathered together in my name, there am I in the midst of them" (Matthew 18:20).

When Ozanam died in 1853, there were already an astonishing two thousand Society conferences or chapters in twenty-nine countries in Europe, North America, and the Middle East.[40]

In the twentieth century, Pope Paul VI revealed he was a Vincentian.[41]

Today the organization has nearly one million volunteers worldwide whose mission is to visit the poor in their homes—whether home is a house, apartment, motel room, shack, car, or porch step. They might meet homeless clients at coffee shops or church offices.

Yet this global society is one of the best-kept secrets of the Catholic Church. If you ask the average Catholic, he probably couldn't tell you who Frederic Ozanam was, or what the Society is really all about. The most likely response is "They run thrift stores and collect clothes and furniture for the poor." Or "That's an organization for seniors."

Hardly. The Society welcomes anyone eighteen and older. You could be a Vincentian while still in high school and experience a transformational change in your life. And if you're eighty, it's not too late to join, either.

What is the essence of the organization? Two Vincentian volunteers sit down with the needy person or family, and see the face of Christ in them.

Often Jesus is hungry and wounded.

These volunteers rely on church poor box donations to help prevent homelessness and utility shutoffs. They buy beds for poor families and fill other basic needs.

Despite this assistance, when you're poor "the wolf" will soon be back at your door. The real miracles occur during conversations between these Christian service workers and their needy friends. The relationships that develop are inspiring. This goes on all over the world, every day.

"The poor are there," said Ozanam. "We should fall down at their feet and say to them: for us, you are the holy images of the God we cannot see, and, not knowing any other way of loving Him, we love Him in you."[42]

That's radical thinking unless you remember Matthew 25.

You see, the spiritual growth of these volunteers is just as important as assisting the needy. Consider these uncommon words from their patron, St. Vincent de Paul: "My friend, you belong to God.

Let this reality color your entire existence. Give yourself up to God ceaselessly with every beat of your heart."[43]

Blessed Frederic Ozanam did just that. Do you think he ever imagined he would have almost one million followers more than 180 years later? His legacy is remarkable. And today, because he replaced words with actions, the things he said are alive and well, inspiring his followers worldwide, at meetings and in prayers.

What will your legacy be?

Who will be the next Frederic Ozanam or Mother Teresa?

Could it be you?

Why not contact your parish Christian Service Commission tomorrow and begin serving your neighbors through an outreach ministry? Until you try it you'll never know the joy and humility of delivering a basket of food to a hungry family, phoning a lonely parishioner once a week, or driving an elderly person to church.

Perhaps helping immigrants and refugees is your calling. Some parishes have campaigns to serve them and make them feel welcome.

Catholic parishes offer many very practical and powerful lay ministries. There's one that's right for you—right under your nose.

Will you invite a friend to join you? How about involving your whole family?

Or could you start a new outreach at your parish, high school, or university?

Remember, Ozanam was just *an inexperienced college kid* when he launched a revolutionary lay vocation.

He was very much in touch with his mortality, too. Ozanam once said, "What poor creatures we are! We do not know if we shall be alive tomorrow, yet we are anxious to know what we shall be doing twenty years hence."[44] Coincidentally, he died just *twenty years* after founding the Society. He was only forty years old.

But at age twenty, it was blunt criticism—the suggestion he was a poser—that stirred the future lawyer and professor to admit the truth about himself, life, and death. Until that fateful day, he was all talk, like many of us. When confronted with this reality, Ozanam quickly acknowledged his need to do something, fast. His credibility and his eternity were at stake.

So now, what's your excuse?

Let's be frank. What do you do besides talk to prove the faith you claim is in you?

EIGHT

Cards for Lazarus

It's been a long, dark winter. So bleak, our postal carrier thought I was dead.

Let me explain.

Record-setting low temps, slippery roads, and endless snow made traveling to Ellen's frequent doctor appointments challenging. I did the driving since an incision in her right groin, the donor site for tissue used in her breast reconstruction, was slow to heal. It was uncomfortable for her to sit without pain medication. Surgeon, plastic surgeon, oncologist, internist, and breast cancer specialty shop— visiting all these experts reshuffled our lives, forcing us out of our comfort zone and into a new, unpredictable schedule.

Chemo starts next week, just five days before Ellen's birthday. She's having her head shaved this weekend and will come home wearing a wig. Why? Because otherwise her real hair would likely start falling out a couple weeks after her first infusion. The eyebrows may hang around a little while longer. The good news is that the whole chemo ordeal should be over after twelve weekly treatments, each one lasting about four hours. God willing, she'll require just IV meds after that, assuming everything goes as planned.

We'd been away from home so often during the day that I had occasionally failed to clear the snow from the walk before dark. Or my snow removal wasn't up to the usual standard. Thankfully one of our neighbors shoveled it for us sometimes.

The cancer care had us breaking so many of life's routines that our long-time postal worker, Pam, surmised I had passed away. Seriously! She was so convinced of my sudden demise that she asked a neighbor if I had died.

You couldn't really blame her, because I work from home and typically take daily walks and bike rides during my lunch break. Even in the dead of winter, I speed walk. Pam has seen me exercising religiously for many years. But the last few months have hardly been normal.

Pam hadn't yet heard about Ellen's illness when—day after day, week after week—she walked to our porch sorting through greeting cards addressed to Mrs. Ellen Stepien. Then she'd pick up the smaller thank-you cards from our mailbox, with Ellen's handwriting on the envelopes. Pam figured she was delivering sympathy cards and I must have been lying in the icy turf on the hill in the tiny cemetery up the road.

We had a good laugh today when she finally spotted me alive and walking up the sidewalk. After she confessed her concern, she shared a serious anecdote. "I had another house once where I was delivering all these greeting cards," Pam explained. "When I asked the woman, 'Is it your birthday?' she said, 'No. My husband died.'" From that day on, Pam never asked that question again.

Little did she know, she was delivering dozens of love notes to our house. Mass cards from family and friends, personal letters full of prayer and hope for Ellen. Perhaps she also saw people driving up and ducking inside our front door with meals, or the express delivery driver carrying packages, and florists with arrangements. She may have even observed a priest bearing flowers and a retiree bringing the Holy Eucharist.

Never before have I felt so much of God's love through other people. The outpouring of support and calories was beyond our imagination. There was a steady stream of homemade casseroles, soups, pastas, cookies, cakes, and muffins. In addition we were blessed with French crock ice cream, chocolates, exotic teas with a teapot, whole baskets overflowing with goodies, perfume, a handmade pink prayer shawl, blankets, pajamas and loungewear, a certificate for a massage, videos, books, and too many comforting phone calls to remember.

For me, the emotional lift was unforgettable. I can only imagine the courage it gave Ellen. The gratitude gushed from her pen, and the sincere thank-you notes quickly replaced the fatigue, pain, and uncertainty. Even though she would soon be bald, Ellen had to be confident that God really did number the hairs on her head (see Luke 12:7).

Gratitude is the fountain of faith. It has the unique capability of humbling us while elevating our souls. When we count our blessings and acknowledge their source, the warmth we feel is God's unconditional love for us. It's always there, even when we're convinced that we're in control and making all our own breaks.

But if you really want to experience what God must feel like when we're grateful, open a sincere thank-you letter from a poor person. Have you ever received one? Ask people who serve the needy. They get them all the time.

Two parishioners were visiting a mother and her teenage daughter. This working mom faced a messy pile of bills and had to choose which to pay and which to delay. Dad was out of the picture and not contributing any child support. The young woman had typed the following and slipped it into the stack of debts, as a much-needed reminder:

> Blessings come in disguise. . . . What we have planned isn't always God's plan. . . . His plan may be better than what we ever imagined despite the situation. . . . Somehow we always survive. . . . Life's experiences teach us to trust in God. It always works out. . . . He gives us what we need . . . not want.

Below the neatly typed prose was this hand-scrawled list:

Utilities
Tuition
Mortgage
Water
Phone
Car Fixed
Doctors
Dentist
Attorney

Can you imagine reading those words after getting to know the family and hearing them express their joy for the assistance they received? In the middle of winter, a parish ministry helped restore heat to their home after it had been shut off.

Then there was the mother staying temporarily in a motel room with her two young children. The experience of interacting with this family was indescribable for her two Christian volunteers. More than tears and true confessions, they witnessed unshakable faith. It's challenging to understand how a parent can seem fearless when only hope in God stands between the family and life in a shelter. With a little financial assistance, this working mom was able to get the kids to school, keep them warm and safe, and work her full-time job. She expressed her sheer joy and prayers of praise in this personal poem she penned to her friends from the local church:

> I will never be able to thank you
> for all you've done.
> You gave me so much hope
> when I had none.
> I thank God every day for bringing
> you to me,
> and for opening my eyes to make me see
> that life is not all dark—there is light,
> and that it is time to make things right.
> I am a better person just for knowing you.
> Thank you so much for all that you do.
> You helped mend my soul and my heart
> When they both had been broken apart.

Her courage and grace in the face of serious issues and humiliation reminds us of our own vulnerability, our own need to say, "Thank you, Lord."

Remember how only one of the ten lepers came back to Jesus to express gratitude for his healing? Jesus asked where the other nine were (see Luke 17:17). When was the last time you really expressed thanks to God?

When we say grace before meals, do we remember to pray for those who are hungry? Those trying to keep a roof over their heads?

Those who are suffering have a knack for finding great joy in little blessings. Take, for instance, a man just paroled from prison who was desperate for a job. On a follow-up phone call with his Christian visitors, he shared his heart: "Even if you couldn't help me, I was grateful for the time you spent with me. It made me happy."

Loneliness is solitary confinement without bars. The key to freedom is you and me.

Now, undeniably many of the poor are victims of the choices they make. That's true for each of us. But we don't all begin life from the same starting line. We don't choose our parents; we don't choose where or when we are born. Adopted and foster kids don't pick their parents, either.

As we take our first breaths, some of us are blessed with much more than others. Two caring parents. A safe home and neighborhood. A healthy mind and body. Good role models. Nurturing schools. A sense of reliable routines and security. A consistent, rich faith life. And most of all, love. It conquers all.

Some born into challenging situations owe their success to compassionate teachers, coaches, mentors, and spiritual directors—including priests, nuns, and deacons. These servants bothered to take the time to shepherd young lambs.

Poverty is a complex blend of underemployment, joblessness, chronic illness, disabilities, dependence, mental illness, addiction, illiteracy, and greed. We were not all raised in stable families with moms, dads, and grandparents who could teach us faith, the basics of financial literacy, or how to be healthy.

And not everyone can afford the things we regard as the basics. Consider these comments from needy parents hoping for something better:

- "I know my kids are getting nutrition, because they're eating bologna sandwiches at school."
- "I have plenty of canned food; it would be great if I could just get some meat."
- "It would be nice to have fresh fruit and vegetables."

Yet it's not money and resources the poor miss the most. Even Jesus says we don't live on bread alone; we need heavenly nutrition from the Word of God (see Luke 4:4). And indeed, what the poor crave is a sense that they genuinely matter, at least as much as the dogs and cats in the local animal shelter. (We might think of groups like the Society of St. Vincent DePaul, Catholic Relief Services, and Habitat for Humanity as the humane societies for stray men and women.)

Diane had lost a job as a caretaker, and part of her wages included room and board. She needed help with her car insurance and her monthly storage fee. Otherwise, she would lose most of her possessions. She was now living in her car. "Getting fired hurt me," she exclaimed through her tears. "I made $18,000 last year. I believe God will take care of me. It would be a miracle if I could get these two bills paid."

Despite her tenuous situation, Diane found peace in the Christian service workers who sat down with her. They shared some snacks and ended their meeting with a prayer. Diane shared:

God is at my side. Praying just now . . . comfort came over
me. St. Paul kept his faith when his ship was wrecked. Every
time something goes wrong, God opens another door for me.

Anyone who works directly with the poor knows they can be inspiring. They are profoundly grateful for the simplest kindness.

Have you ever had a poor person serve you or offer you food?
Invariably those who visit the needy discover their mind-boggling
generosity. One Muslim refugee from the Middle East brought his
Christian guest a tumbler of fresh orange juice on a tray. Nearby,
the client's two developmentally disabled daughters played on the
floor. A mother who had returned from the local church food pantry found herself with more fresh fruit than her family could use.
"Would you like some?" she asked her guests from the neighborhood
church. "I have too many apples."

How many times have you visited people of means and not received a glass of water? How many gifts have you sent to family,
friends, or business associates that were never acknowledged?

When the poor receive a grocery store gift certificate or some
help with a job search, they say things like:

- "I'm too blessed to be depressed."
- "Oh, thank you! You are my God-mom and God-pop."
- "I have never had a total stranger care about me so much."
- "I've been praying and praying. God knows what you
  need even before you ask, but this is tough. My son pays
  $100 a week for gas to get to work. I tell him, don't give
  up, son, at least you're doing the right thing and you have
  a job."

These are spontaneous comments from real people, proving poverty is a powerful teacher—both for those in need and those of us with too much. Remember, St. Francis of Assisi referred to "Lady Poverty," and he "married" her.

People who serve Christ through the poor find it difficult to avoid friendships with them. They begin praying daily for the people they've met. They make an effort to keep in touch. Sometimes their poor friends send *them* gifts! One wife and mother sent a small Christmas gift to her Christian patrons. It was an etched mirror that read: "Faith is being sure of what we hope for and certain of what we do not see" (Hebrews 11:1). How's that for seeing the reflection of Jesus in the poor?

And the needy are shamelessly ready to share special moments and events with their guests. The disabled man was living with his brother and sister-in-law when he was first visited by two Christian service volunteers. Being the third wheel was a tough, embarrassing situation for Fred. He was an adult, living in his brother's basement.

About a year later, Fred was delighted to see his visitors from church again and to share a hug. They had all talked on the phone over the past months but hadn't seen each other in a while. Fred was so proud of his new apartment, and he insisted on giving his guests a tour. It was very tidy, and he explained that he was a bit compulsive about keeping it clean.

His half-dozen garments hung neatly in a row in his closet. Fred picked up a dress shoe to reveal that it had a hole in the sole. He was even proud about that, because it represented the many miles he had walked and the weight he'd lost.

His bills were up-to-date, and he was receiving regular treatment for a chronic illness. Fred was grateful to God for all the ways he was fulfilling his needs. He confessed that he was once so poor, he was forced to sell a pair of old cufflinks on the street. One man reached under his car seat and pulled out a full bottle of dishwashing liquid to offer as a trade—suds for jewelry. Coincidentally, soap was one of the items on Fred's shopping list!

"God gives me exactly what I need . . . when I need it," he said.

This is a Christian success story. The burdens of poverty and chronic illness remain. But, like Fred, we can feel joy and hope and a sense of serenity that only God can give. Even if we only experience this peaceful place for a little while, if we can string enough of those days together, life has real meaning. It can make us smile inside and out, and feel fulfilled, regardless of our circumstances. And that goes for the needy people we might help, as well as those of us who are financially secure but still searching for something more. Much more.

Serenity is true happiness found in the footsteps of Christ on a journey to the everlasting. And when we do our best to follow the Lord and his saints, we go places we never dreamed.

As Mike did. He was a seasoned, industrious factory worker raising a family with his wife. Yet Mike found time to serve in his parish. He was quite active, working all the clothing drives and pitching in on special projects whenever possible.

Then Carl came into Mike's life. Carl had fallen off his bike riding through the ice and snow to his job at a local grocery chain. With a broken arm, he couldn't work. Carl was living in a motel, and without his weekly paycheck, he'd be out on the street in a few days.

Mike and another volunteer, Joe, talked to Carl's boss. Yep, the story checked out. Carl was a hardworking stock person who rarely missed his shift. The manager confided that Carl suffered from mental illness and would have crying spells from time to time. He also liked to imitate Elvis Presley, combing his jet-black hair like the king of rock-and-roll.

This would not be an easy case. Carl would be out of work with no disability insurance for a few months. His food stamps totaled fourteen dollars per week. Yes, you read that right. Two dollars a day. Because he had a job, that's all he received. Carl was the definition of the working poor. Fortunately the volunteer organization had enough money in their treasury to pay his motel bill and help with food until he could recover.

Like many clients, Carl offered to volunteer in order to repay his debt.

Mike soon discovered that his new friend also had heart disease, after rushing him to the local emergency room. He began driving Carl to cardiology and psychiatry appointments. He helped Carl find a therapist he could relate to. Then Mike learned the police were responding to disturbances at Carl's motel, night after night. He pursued a low cost apartment for Carl and found a futon for him. Mike helped him move and clean up his new, safer place. They had lots of laughs together.

Mike and Carl became friends. They both loved reruns of *The Three Stooges*. Although not Catholic, Carl began coming to Mass and sitting with Mike and Joe. From time to time, he'd cry in church, but he now had friends to console him. By the time Mass was over, he'd be smiling as he walked out with his new pals.

When spring arrived, Carl's arm had healed. He returned to work and once again rode his bike to the grocery store. It was a longer trip from his new apartment, but he was living in a very clean, secure neighborhood, with a wonderful park right next door. He could afford to pay the rent with his paycheck—it was actually cheaper than the seedy motel.

Sadly Carl's heart disease worsened. One day Mike learned that Carl had died. His family lived in another state, and they expressed gratitude for all Mike had done to support Carl, who had struggled his entire adult life.

Mike and his fellow volunteers mourned the loss of Carl, but they were relieved to know he was finally at peace with the Lord. He was undoubtedly loved. And they had seen him smile and laugh many times. Carl had been happy.

Do you have any needy friends who are now in heaven?

Mike does. And he is always grateful he met Carl.

Jesus shares a parallel story with many twists and a surprise ending. His is the parable about the rich man and Lazarus (see Luke 16:19–31). The wealthy fellow lived well, dressed in nothing but the best, and ate like a king. His neighbor, Lazarus, begged for scraps of food, but the rich man didn't help. Sometimes he would open the door of his fancy digs, only to find Lazarus sleeping on his front steps—just as some of the homeless do today. Only back in Jesus' day, there were no soup kitchens or shelters. Lazarus was a beggar.

What did the wealthy man do? He stepped right over Lazarus and went about his business. He never bothered to share his table scraps. Even the stray dogs felt compassion for the poor man and licked his sores.

When Lazarus passed away, the angels carried him to the bosom of Father Abraham. He was now in eternity, without pain and suffering. He rested his head on Abraham's shoulder. The love he felt fulfilled all his needs.

One day the rich man died. His family and servants buried him in the ground. He received no heavenly escort. In fact, he woke up in "the netherworld." It was an unpleasant place where he was always thirsty, never satisfied. The rich man looked up and saw someone he recognized. It was Lazarus, the beggar he had ignored his whole life. What was he doing in the bosom of Abraham?

The rich man felt slighted, overlooked. He cried out to Father Abraham, begging for mercy. And now he had a job to offer Lazarus. Would Abraham please tell Lazarus to fetch the suffering man a drink, just a few drops of water on his parched tongue? The netherworld was a relentlessly hot place.

But Abraham said no. It was something the rich man wasn't used to hearing. Abraham explained that Lazarus had spent his life in poverty, while the rich man had never gone without. In the afterlife, their situations were reversed. Besides, Abraham added, there was a "no-fly zone" between them that could not be crossed. Lazarus couldn't travel to the netherworld, and the rich man couldn't visit Lazarus.

This was no "Scrooge" story with a happy ending. There wouldn't be any ghosts of Passover past, present, and future. It was too late to be redeemed. For the first time in many years, the rich man felt a sense of urgency about his relationship with God. He hoped there was still time to do something good for those he loved. He wanted to save his family from the netherworld.

Jesus finishes the parable with this dialogue between the rich man and Abraham as they spoke across the mammoth, impassable chasm.

"I beg you, father, send [Lazarus] to my father's house, for I have five brothers, so that he may warn them, lest they also come into this place of torment."

But Abraham said, "They have Moses and the prophets; let them hear them."

And he said, "No, father Abraham; but if some one goes to them from the dead, they will repent."

Then [Abraham] said to him, 'If they do not hear Moses and the prophets, neither will they be convinced if some one should rise from the dead." (Luke 16:27–31)

It's true. No matter how many times the Lord touches our lives with blessings. No matter how many of our loved ones die. No matter how many tragedies we witness among the marginalized masses. We step over the warning signs in our doorways. Glance away from the bodies in the news. Avoid the needy on the sidewalks of life like they are so many fire hydrants and lampposts along the way.

What kind of greeting cards will be in your mailbox tomorrow?

Will you be around to open them?

Wherever you are, will you be happy?

NINE

Puff of Smoke

"In my Father's house there are many dwelling places. If there were not, would I have told you that I am going to prepare a place for you?" (John 14:2)

Many residences in one house? Enough room in heaven for all the Lord's followers? Sounds like Jesus' Dad lives on a sprawling estate in an unimaginable palace.

And St. Paul confirmed that Jesus graciously sacrificed that grand mansion and infinite wealth so we could have it. That's the mind of God. "For your sake he became poor although he was rich, so that by his poverty you might become rich" (2 Corinthians 8:9).

What a gift! God chose to live, toil, sweat, bleed, and die in our world. He hung out with sinners and called them friends. Why? So we could become family and inherit his kingdom. He wants us to live with him, here and after we die. Always happy. Permanently in a relationship.

Jesus came to share his wealth, to pay all our debts. But he didn't buy our salvation with cash or priceless bling. St. Paul says we became rich *by the Lord's poverty*.

Wait, what? Poverty is a good thing?

Jesus was "all in" from his birth in Bethlehem, trading a celestial throne for a manger. He gave everything for us, including his human life. So the Lord certainly was justified when he told the rich young man to sell his stuff, give the proceeds to the poor, and follow him. He was simply asking him to do what he had already done himself. No hypocrisy in this request.

Our God-made-man Messiah set the example in many ways. The way he quietly endured, simply and humbly. The way he loved, deeply and mercifully—feeding, consoling, and healing. Defending sinners. Preventing stoning and blunting criticism. The way he washed feet at the Last Supper, a role model for his disciples. Even the way he washed the feet of his betrayer, Judas. The way he forgave, while persecuted, smacked, whipped, spit upon, mocked, and crucified.

He is *the* way.

The Lord spent much of his ministry talking about the poor, helping them and validating them as being important in the kingdom of God. This is not what people in his day expected of the Messiah. No wonder they didn't recognize him. In fact St. John the Baptist told his disciples to ask Jesus if he was the "one to come." And Jesus confirmed that he was indeed the fulfillment of the prophecies. He was more than the second coming of the prophet Elijah. He was the Christ, the Messiah.

"Go and tell John what you have seen and heard: the blind regain their sight, the lame walk, lepers are cleansed, the deaf hear, the dead are raised, the poor have the good news proclaimed to them. And blessed is the one who takes no offense at me." (Luke 7:22–23)

Jesus knew many people would be offended—appalled by his emphasis of the marginalized. Shocking! The Messiah would not be about worldly might, wealth, glory, and nationalism. He even told his fellow Israelites to pay Roman taxes!

It's no surprise that today some folks react the same way to Christ's gospel of poverty.

Why did God become poor when he became man? The answer is in his Word. "No one can serve two masters. He will either hate one and love the other, or be devoted to one and despise the other. You cannot serve God and mammon" (Matthew 6:24).

Mammon is an ancient Aramaic word that means "wealth" or "property." So our Lord is saying, very directly, that we can't serve God and our 401K investments equally. Our careers. Our decorator homes. Our lawns and gardens. Our spots in the limelight. None of these can be our master.

How many masters do you have?

Money is a tool. But hoarding it far beyond our reasonable need can become an obsession. And the desire to accumulate is itself an idol that we worship and honor with an unwillingness to share.

Are you a cheerful giver?

Do you have a healthy fear (awe) of the Lord, or are you more afraid of losing your net worth or social status?

Greed is the love of money. It causes us to serve our bank balance, our reputation, our ego, and our reservoir of precious, invaluable time—instead of serving God.

Who do you love most? Yourself?

What do you love? Why?

In the Gospel of Luke, the Lord continues to discourage the hypocrisy of those who idolize mammon.

> The Pharisees, who loved money, heard all these things and sneered at him. And he said to them, "You justify yourselves in the sight of others, but God knows your hearts; for what is of human esteem is an abomination in the sight of God." (Luke 16:14–15)

"Abomination"? Some Bible translations say "detestable" or "loathsome." According to Jesus, when we glorify wealth and soak up public praise, God finds that evil and repulsive. In turn, the Pharisees, who adored riches and public acclaim, saw Jesus as revolting. They turned up their noses at him, because they found God's Word ugly and repugnant.

The Lord tells us that it's incredibly difficult for a rich person to enter the kingdom of God. And in some way we're all wealthy, clinging to our earthly treasures, choosing them over Jesus, the way.

The gate to heaven is a narrow one, too tight for lots of perishable cargo. The baggage fees are a killer. Unless I drop the stuff I'm hanging onto—material, emotional, and spiritual burdens—I won't fit through the opening. And in God's eyes, I'll look hideous covered in all that gaudy human esteem. An abomination, stuck in the pearly gates.

Standing at my headstone, will the Lord be mourning or rejoicing?

If heaven published your death notice today, how would it read?

Will your eulogy spark a party among the angels and saints—or inspire fond memories for your broker or banker?

Jesus says we have to choose between serving our heavenly trust fund or our earthly stash. We can't do both.

"Do not store up for yourselves treasures on earth, where moth and decay destroy, and thieves break in and steal. But store up treasures in heaven, where neither moth nor decay destroys, nor thieves break in and steal. For where your treasure is, there also will your heart be." (Matthew 6:19–21)

Where is my heart? What am I storing up? What are my motives?

When Jesus spoke these words, many of those who heard them were permanently transformed. For example, after he died, rose, and ascended into heaven, Christ's followers were the foundation of the early Church. The Acts of the Apostles is a record of how they lived. Like their master, they shared liberally and joyfully.

All who believed were together and had all things in common; they would sell their property and possessions and divide them among all according to each one's need. (Acts 2:44–45)

Was this socialism? Communism? Communal living?

It was Christianity. The original Church—the growing and thriving body of Christ, led by people who had actually heard Jesus speak, who had personally experienced his miracles and resurrection.

The Apostles Peter, James, and John were exceptionally close to Jesus. He invited them exclusively to hang out with him and witness his Transfiguration. But as the Messiah agonized and prayed in the garden just hours before his trial and crucifixion, Peter, James, and John dozed nearby.

When the Lord first recruited these three men to join his ministry, they were in the fishing business. Simon, who Jesus nicknamed "Peter," was a hardy, type-A personality. The outspoken wild man became pope number one. If he were alive today, he'd probably own an old Harley and ride without a helmet. Peter tried to walk on water with Jesus in a gale; he wanted to build monuments to Jesus, Moses, and Elijah at the Transfiguration for the Jewish Feast of Tabernacles. Peter drew his sword to defend the Lord in the Garden of Gethsemane. He was a doer. A rock 'n' roll kind of guy. Hence the nickname "Rock" and the papal job description.

James and John were brothers, poised to inherit their dad's seafood concession in Galilee. And they had serious ambition. Once they actually asked Jesus to grant them the privilege of sitting on his right and his left when they reached his glory (see Mark 10:37). Think about what they were asking. They aspired to unimaginable greatness and a stratospherically lofty position. They were genuine entrepreneurs with big dreams.

However, in time, as these three fishermen shadowed the Lord down dusty roads, they learned the truth about life, death, and real treasure. They learned about love.

Peter, the first pope, wrote this advice to the early Church:

> Finally, all of you, be of one mind, sympathetic, loving toward one another, compassionate, humble. Do not return evil for evil, or insult for insult; but, on the contrary, a blessing, because to this you were called, that you might inherit a blessing.
> (1 Peter 3:8–9)

This came from the guy who slashed off a foe's ear during Jesus' arrest. Peter went through quite a personal conversion.

John was the beloved disciple. Among other things, he was known for resting his head on Jesus' chest during the Last Supper.

He could listen to the Lord's heart beating, his voice resonating from within. John defined God as love, a love that is only at home in the merciful. He wrote:

> Do not love the world or the things of the world. If anyone loves the world, the love of the Father is not in him. For all that is in the world, sensual lust, enticement for the eyes, and a pretentious life, is not from the Father but is from the world. Yet the world and its enticement are passing away. But whoever does the will of God remains forever. (1 John 2:15–17)

> If someone who has worldly means sees a brother in need and refuses him compassion, how can the love of God remain in him? Children, let us love not in word or speech but in deed and truth. (1 John 3:17–18)

How truthful is your love? How unconditional is it?

What are you doing to bring Christ to others?

Do you look for Jesus in all those you meet?

The Lord said, "Do to others whatever you would have them do to you" (Matthew 7:12). How carefully do we follow that "Golden Rule?" Do we tenderly apply that command? Are we golden—or are our actions just gold-plated?

St. Peter said our faith in Jesus is more precious than gold (see 1 Peter 1:7). As rugged as he was on land and sea, it's not surprising that he spoke about Christian love and mercy as a forceful shield to wield against evil—a tool to be leveraged to serve neighbors and express gratitude to God.

Above all, let your love for one another be intense, because love covers a multitude of sins. Be hospitable to one another without complaining. As each one has received a gift, use it to serve one another as good stewards of God's varied grace. (1 Peter 4:8–10)

Scholars attribute the Book of Revelation to the disciple John. It includes this warning from Jesus to laid-back Christians, those merely going through the motions. In Revelation, the Lord compares their complacency to a tasteless meal:

I know your works; I know that you are neither cold nor hot. I wish you were either cold or hot. So, because you are lukewarm, neither hot nor cold, I will spit you out of my mouth. For you say, "I am rich and affluent and have no need of anything," and yet do not realize that you are wretched, pitiable, poor, blind, and naked. (Revelation 3:15–17)

When it comes to our faith, are we on fire, ablaze with the Holy Spirit? Or are we cool customers, so low-key most don't know we're Christians? Or are we just tepid, trying to have it both ways? Are we hedging our bets on God?

St. James is the author of the famous "faith versus works" epistle. He begins his five-chapter epistle by describing himself as "a slave of God and the Lord Jesus Christ." James became the Bishop of Jerusalem, and St. Paul identified him as one of the "pillars" of the early Church (see Galatians 2:9).

In the first century, as early as 47 A.D., James wrote to the Christian community scattered far and wide. He passionately begged believers to do more than believe, but to behave as followers of Christ—not posers.

> What good is it, my brothers, if someone says he has faith but does not have works? Can that faith save him?·If a brother or sister has nothing to wear and has no food for the day, and one of you says to them, "Go in peace, keep warm, and eat well," but you do not give them the necessities of the body, what good is it? So also faith of itself, if it does not have works, is dead. (James 2:14–17)

Is your faith on life support? Do you talk about serving people or do you actually do it? Do you act on your words, thoughts, and promises?

With an eerie timelessness, James issued a wake-up call regarding our mortality and the fleeting nature of wealth.

> Come now, you who say, "Today or tomorrow we shall go into such and such a town spend a year there doing business, and make a profit"—you have no idea what your life will be like tomorrow. You are a puff of smoke that appears briefly and then disappears. Instead you should say, "If the Lord wills it, we shall live to do this or that." (James 4:13–15)

A puff of smoke! If the Lord wills it, I shall live. Hauntingly wise words from someone who watched his Messiah crucified for his goodness at thirty-three years old.

Is ego and ambition obscuring your view of reality?

Do you make your luck, or are you grateful for your blessings?

Do you acknowledge that God is in control of your universe, or do you believe that you build your success?

Do you accept your mortality, your puff-of-smoke, dust-to-dust nature?

The rock band Kansas echoed St. James' sentiments in the 1978 smash hit song "Dust in the Wind," from the *Point of No Return* album.

Guitarist Kerry Livgren wrote the words and the tune, describing each of us as particles blowing in a breeze—with no ability to control the clock or delay death, no matter how wealthy we are. Reading Native American poetry influenced his lyrics. Then in 1980 Livgren became a Christian, acknowledging that his songwriting had been part of his spiritual search for something more and that his fame and fortune were temporary—just as life is for all of us.[45]

Death is the great equalizer. It puts everyone on the same level. No thrones or pedestals, no matter how fancy your funeral.

Likewise, the letters of St. James to the early Christians offer very specific spiritual insights on our attitudes about social and economic status. As in today's churches, James' congregation had members who shopped at thrift stores and those who came to Mass flashing their jewels and expensive clothing. Income inequality has always been around.

For if a man with gold rings on his fingers and in fine clothes comes into your assembly, and a poor person in shabby clothes also comes in, and you pay attention to the one wearing the fine clothes and say, "Sit here, please," while you say to the poor one,

"Stand there," or "Sit at my feet," have you not made distinctions among yourselves and become judges with evil designs? Listen, my beloved brothers. Did not God choose those who are poor in the world to be rich in faith and heirs of the kingdom that he promised to those who love him? (James 2:2–5)

Do we welcome the poor in today's Church? Do we offer privilege to donors? Are the poor a priority, or do we simply pity them?

James even warned the wealthy against exploiting laborers and abusing good people:

Behold, the wages you withheld from the workers who harvested your fields are crying aloud, and the cries of the harvesters have reached the ears of the Lord of hosts. You have lived on earth in luxury and pleasure; you have fattened your hearts for the day of slaughter. You have condemned; you have murdered the righteous one; he offers you no resistance. (James 5:4–6)

Do we enjoy cheap goods made by underpaid laborers? Do we negotiate unfair deals so we can relish our gains? Do we profit from violence, destruction, and mayhem? Do we abuse our rank and power and step on the little guy?

When I read James, sometimes it's as though he's alive, blogging about our current times. Then I remember the human condition is what it is and always has been. As Jesus said, "The spirit is willing, but the flesh is weak" (Matthew 26:41).

So how do we get stronger?

Today many people are concerned about the right to life. Abortion. Capital punishment. End-of-life issues. Unjust war. These serious matters spur some to serve God with passionate words. Others are moved by the spirit to flex their heart muscles and wash feet, even in very unpleasant, intimidating places.

The movie *Dead Man Walking* was based on the 1982 true story and starred Sean Penn as Patrick Sonnier, a vicious, convicted murderer of two teenagers. The court sentenced him to die in the electric chair in Louisiana's Angola State Prison. Susan Sarandon played the role of Sister Helen Prejean, the real-life Roman Catholic nun and spiritual advisor to Sonnier. She ministered to him while he counted his days on death row. Sister Prejean also comforted the victims' families and counseled the prison staff as they wrestled with their job description as executioners. Although she couldn't undo Sonnier's sentence, Sister Prejean brought unprecedented attention to the issue of capital punishment. This gut-wrenching story inspired a national best-selling book, a movie, a stage play, an opera, and a music album. But more importantly, the compassionate nun was able to bring the Lord's love to all involved in the tragedy of murder and the vengeful death penalty.[46]

In 2015, Sister Prejean made headlines again, advocating for leniency in the trial of convicted Boston Marathon bomber, Dzhokhar Tsarnaev. She testified to help spare Tsarnaev's life, seeking mercy for the unmerciful, even though it was an intensely unpopular cause.

The Catholic Church, led by the United States Conference of Catholic Bishops (USCCB), is speaking out to end unfair sentencing for youth who are often tried as adults in some states. These "juvies" need mentors.

Could you become a big brother or big sister to a convicted kid? Visit? Write? Befriend? Share your gifts?

In "The Sheep and the Goats Clause," Jesus specifically mentions visiting the jailed four times (see Matthew 25:36, 39, 43, 44). He wants us to liberate the captives with love.

A man in my parish regularly visits women in prison. He's participated in this ministry for years, and it has changed him and his friends behind bars. Another friend is writing letters to a convict, at the suggestion of her pastor. She has a pen pal at the state pen.

Remember, "where two or three are gathered in his name . . ." (Matthew 18:20).

On the gritty streets of Detroit and its surrounding, comfortable suburbs, you can find the Guadalupe Workers defending young lives. Leaders Edmund Miller and Alicia Wong are black-belt sidewalk counselors who gently but fervently stand guard at abortion clinics. Miller has been on the streets with his Catholic life-saving ministry since 1987. And his team has recruited others to help—ordinary people like you and me. Together they work tirelessly to convince "abortion-minded" mothers to keep their babies. Their faithful presence, Saturday after Saturday, month after month, year after year, has saved many lives—both babies in the flesh and parents in the spirit. One doctor was even forced to shut down an abortion practice because the Guadalupe volunteers persuaded so many mothers to choose life. That eroded the physician's revenues until he was evicted for unpaid rent.[47]

Evangelizing and ministering in pairs, the Guadalupe Workers provide peaceful, law-abiding, diligent Christian compassion, quietly burning as a bright light of truth amidst those who fear the unknown future of their lives and the lives growing inside them. The Guadalupes are not antagonistic. On the contrary, they simply offer love and support.

Some of the Guadalupes are married. Some are engineers. Some are philosophers. Some are churchgoers who realized that attending Mass wasn't enough. Some have come for a decade. Some drive in from neighboring states. Some are parents; some are teachers. Some battle personal hardships and disease. They all make time to protect the unborn by showing mercy to the parents planning to abort them.

And if the Guadalupes succeed in persuading a pregnant mother or couple to keep the baby, they don't consider their work done. Funded by donations, this pro-life ministry assists with ultrasounds and other medical care, if needed. Volunteers drive expectant mothers to doctor appointments. They buy diapers, provide beds, pay rent and utility bills, and stock pantries. They house families and develop relationships with them to help ensure that they thrive. In some cases, the connections and support last for years. So does the love.[48]

Don't forget, as St. James said, it's not enough to encourage those in need to succeed and be healthy; we must help and serve them in ways that make a real difference in their lives.

What does pro-life mean to you?

Are you consistently pro-life?

Is this something you talk about or do you actually invest your time in prayer and service to those who are suffering?

How much of your valuable time would you give to save a life?

Comfort a prisoner of loneliness?

Coach a fellow sinner, without condemnation, to find peace in a conflict?

Protest or testify against violence and war?

How many seniors do you call or visit on a regular basis?

Even when you're old and disabled, will you call or write to comfort another?

Could you read to the blind?

In the provocative parable, The Good Samaritan, Jesus makes an outcast the hero. Hebrews considered their enemies, the Samaritans, to be heretics. Although Samaritans and Jews both revered the Torah (the first five books of the Bible) they disagreed about most everything else, including where and how to worship. Their ancient rift was born of smoldering regional politics, culminating in a split between the northern tribes of Israel and their royal leader, Jeroboam, versus the south and King Rehoboam of Judah, from the house of David. Hatred and animosity grew over time and their theological differences exploded, lasting many centuries. It was worse than the Hatfields and the McCoys.

Yet, at the end of the parable, Jesus said, "Go and do likewise" (Luke 10:37); he specifically told his listeners to follow the Samaritan's example. Why? Because in the story, it was the heretic who mercifully stopped to rescue the "half-dead" Hebrew victim, whom the robbers left on the side of the road between Jerusalem and Jericho. The whole event takes place in the heart of Hebrew territory.

The Hebrew priest and the Levite had already seen the beaten man, but decided to continue on their way. They had the same choice to make, but they chose not to help. In fact, they walked by on the other side of the street!

Some scholars say the clergymen wanted to avoid touching the man's body, because if he were dead, they would have become ritually impure. For seven days they could not have performed their Temple duties. Others contend rescuing the dying always trumped both ritual purity and Sabbath laws.[49] But whether they viewed themselves as too pious to get their hands dirty, or too important to stoop to aid an unknown victim, Jesus said they made the wrong choice.

On the other hand, the Good Samaritan poured oil and wine on the victim's wounds and bandaged them. He put him on his beast and took him to the nearest inn where he spent the night and tended to the battered guy's needs. But he didn't stop there. The Samaritan was remarkably compassionate. The next day he gave the innkeeper silver coins and promised, on his return trip, to pay any difference to cover his injured guest's expenses (Luke 10:33–35).

Would you do that? Would you rescue a total stranger and treat her like family? Donate a kidney or your bone marrow? Drive someone you don't really know to radiation treatments or chemotherapy?

Today I spoke to Bob, who works at a food pantry. He shared a Good Samaritan story with me. On a freezing day in the middle of winter, a man clad in only flip-flops and wearing all the clothes he owned arrived at a Catholic parish looking for assistance. The food pantry volunteers gave him plenty to eat, but they also provided money for boots and clothing. Their visitor had been evicted; the landlord had kept all his belongings. He needed to find a job.

With his new wardrobe, the man was able to apply for an engineering position at a major global manufacturer. He had a good education but had lost his way. The employer saw his potential and gave him the opportunity. The reinvigorated man called back to tell his church friends that he "wouldn't be needing any more of their help." He now had a good job and wanted to pay them back some day.

Bob and his fellow volunteers were rewarded with a taste of heaven. They had witnessed a miraculous transformation because they decided to volunteer—to stop on the roadside of life to help a victim. To invest some time in the kingdom to come, the place that Jesus calls home.

Again, where two or three are gathered in his name to do his work, Jesus is there.

And with God, all things are possible. Remember the amazing proclamation from the Lord that I shared earlier? "Amen, amen, I say to you, whoever believes in me will do the works that I do, and will do greater ones than these, because I am going to the Father," Jesus says (John 14:12).

It's mind-boggling to consider. How will we do greater things than Jesus? Well, think about it. Together, we can feed millions; cure disease; rescue nations gripped by natural disasters; end oppression and wars and change lives—including our own.

Even rich men and women like us can get into heaven. There are spacious dwellings waiting for you and me in Jesus' kingdom.

Someday we'll all leave this world. Where will you live then, and will you be happy?

TEN

The Dash between the Dates

Today was Ellen's second chemo treatment, and we received devastating news.

The day brought unexpected and grave complications. Not for Ellen, but the fourteen-year-old son of a business colleague and friend. The email that hit my desktop explained that the high school boy had lost his brave battle with a rare form of cancer. He was an inspiringly gifted child, with a heart of gold, taken too early from his parents, brothers, grandmother, extended family, friends, and church community. At the funeral service his Methodist pastor read a letter the boy had written just prior to his confirmation a year earlier. A real believer, he clearly and dearly loved Jesus. The letter described a very sober and conscious decision to be confirmed. Not because his parents wanted it, but because he chose God.

His dad created an online blog about the young man's health ordeal. Ellen sobbed as she read the chronology of his six-month fight. "Why does an old woman like me get to live and a kid has to die?" she cried.

Within two weeks we attended two more funerals. One for a neighbor in his early sixties; he was a generous Catholic who collapsed behind the wheel of his car. This father was scheduled to walk his daughter down the aisle in several months. Although under a doctor's care, there was no prior knowledge of his cardiac condition. But he left an indelible mark on his daughter's heart. Fortunately she had had the maturity and wisdom to use some available time to spend a week vacationing with her dad. A short while later, she was comforting others at his wake.

The third death was the ninety-six-year-old mother of my dear friend, Fr. Joe. Every week until her last, he took his mom to the salon for a little pampering and then out for a light meal. She had been praying for a peaceful passing. God answered her prayers.

Ages fourteen, sixty-three, and ninety-six.

Were their deaths random—or was it their time?

When will your time come?

Are you ready now?

How much time do you figure you have?

Now I lay me down to sleep.

I pray the Lord my soul to keep.

If I should die before I wake.

I pray the Lord my soul to take.

We taught our two sons this children's bedtime prayer when they were small. Most moms and dads don't routinely contemplate losing their children. But it happens everyday in maternity units, cribs, cancer wards, and drive-by shootings in Chicago, Dallas, and Tikrit—as well as on college campuses and battlefields worldwide. Parents, teach your children well and take the lesson to heart. As Psalm 90 says: "Teach us to count our days aright, that we may gain wisdom of heart" (Psalm 90:12).

The summer after my First Holy Communion, one of my classmates was killed. The nuns from my grade school called each student's home to share the news. When I arrived at the funeral parlor, Larry lay in a small casket, wearing his navy blue Communion suit. It was the first time I had seen a dead person. A car had hit my schoolmate just a few days earlier as he dashed across the street.

Little Larry was a spirited kid and a fast runner—the quickest in our class. Reportedly the traffic light was flashing "Don't Walk" as Larry raced across the avenue. He made it!

But his heel caught the curb as the light changed. He fell back onto the road and into oncoming traffic. In the dimly lit funeral home, it was eerie to see Larry lying totally still. It didn't seem quite real. But it was true. Larry's life was over before the third grade.

How many near misses have you and I dodged as we raced through the flashing "Don't Walk" signs of life? We'll never know. People who have health scares can count the obvious ones. Sometimes these experiences give us a new perspective on what's important. Sometimes not.

During her cancer treatments, Ellen has been in contact with Betty, a woman at our church who is fighting to survive. Betty phones us every two weeks or so. She is experiencing a recurrence of breast cancer that has spread. This brave woman is running out of options. A number of clinical trials have rejected her as not being healthy enough.

But Betty has been there for Ellen and me from the start, as soon as people in our church community learned about Ellen's cancer. She calls to check up on my wife, to listen to her concerns, to provide insights about chemo and wigs, and to tell Ellen she's praying for us.

"I want to be like her. I want to be alive when I die," said my cousin Richard when he learned about Betty and her mercy calls. Richard is a retired mortician, ready with a hysterical joke or heart-stopping story from a lifetime of funerals. Betty's unselfishness inspired him.

"Life is just the dash between the dates on your tombstone," he added.

When I think about that wisdom, it helps me understand why I'm here. To fill in the blank. The good old *Baltimore Catechism* taught me that "God made me to know him, to love him, and to serve him in this world, and to be happy with him in the next."[50]

God made me. I am his. That's an everlasting relationship with my Creator that begins at conception.

We're here to serve God and not ourselves? How should we love and serve him?

"The Sheep and the Goats Clause" from Matthew 25 makes it very clear. Jesus wants us to:

- feed
- quench
- clothe

- heal
- visit
- comfort

The Lord calls us to be merciful, even to prisoners. Even to in-laws. But that's not surprising when you think that Jesus himself was:

- homeless
- exiled
- rejected

- humiliated
- convicted
- stripped

- betrayed
- arrested
- jailed
- denied
- beaten
- scourged

- nailed
- mocked
- executed
- lanced
- buried as a pauper

Just as our Master did, our mission is to go to the needy. That's where he hung out when he humbly walked the earth. We are to serve God by searching for him among the lonely, the forgotten, the deprived, and the abandoned.

At a Holy Thursday Mass, my pastor spoke about a memorable T-shirt slogan he'd once seen on a Belgian college student. It read:

Pray
Break Bread
Wash Feet

That's the three-step boogie of Christianity. True Christians let the Lord lead on the dance floor of life, praying and breaking bread with the suffering and then washing their sore feet.

Jesus calls us to do something for the love of God, literally. Something for nothing—something for no worldly gain. Something just to say, "Lord, I love you. Thank you for everything."

Jesus needs nothing from us. Despite giving everything away to pay the ransom for our salvation, he is wealthy beyond imagination. However, his great desire remains that we love him back—with everything we've got. That we follow him so closely we're compelled to die to this world so we can resemble him. St. Paul put it this way:

"For we who live are constantly being given up to death for the sake of Jesus, so that the life of Jesus may be manifested in our mortal flesh" (2 Corinthians 4:11).

When we reach out to the needy—whether they are flat broke or broken despite their material wealth—we have the opportunity to yoke ourselves to Jesus. To walk at his side, step by step, and become gentle and humble like him (see Matthew 11:29).

Suddenly we can begin to see everyone as a brother or sister just as Jesus does. "God does not see as a mortal, who sees the appearance. The Lord looks into the heart" (1 Samuel: 16:7).

When Jesus looks at you and me, he loves us unconditionally, because he sees through our act, our best face and wardrobe, our thoughtless remarks and the pile of clutter in our head. He accepts our:

- fears and insecurities
- self-centeredness and ingratitude
- pride and sense of entitlement
- small-minded behavior and gossip
- immaturity and tantrums
- overindulgence and addictions
- co-dependency and meddling
- laziness and obsessiveness
- judgmental and unforgiving nature
- greed and lust
- grudges and violence
- desire for attention and affection
- willfulness and need to control the world

And after enduring all our ugliness, the Lord finds his way into our hearts where he discovers and plies many soft spots, turning our weaknesses into a supply of beautiful power and strength (see 2 Corinthians 12:9–10). When we welcome him, he stays and builds our:

- courage to turn the other cheek
- empathy
- kindness
- generosity
- thankfulness
- sweetness
- gentleness
- thoughtfulness
- quietness
- mercy

Then when we spend time with those who are hurting, even if they just need companionship in their misery, we can begin to share their pain and acknowledge our own shortcomings and disappointments. Everyone has them. We're all equal. No better, no worse.

By serving others we can learn to embrace our similarities, the good and the bad. Arriving at that place, we can also begin to genuinely count our blessings and accept people as they are. Suddenly that co-worker, in-law, or parishioner who gets on my nerves deserves my compassion and prayers. The person in ripped clothing who smells unclean or appears self-destructive seems more like a hurting neighbor than an irritating stranger.

Each one is someone to love the way God loves us: despite all our warts. That's important to remember when we meet "the underserving poor," those who ask for help but seem to us like they might not warrant it. Sometimes those who visit the homes of the needy discover big screen TVs, tattoos, and cell phones, apparently eating up the family budget.

Many of us also know people who are financially comfortable but have spending addictions. Or others who feel they are entitled to every break, opportunity, VIP freebie, or government benefit—even if they don't need it.

Let's be honest: We're all struggling with something. We all make foolish decisions, financial or otherwise. For example, someone might be a genius with money but a failure at marriage or family relationships. Or great with people but lousy with paperwork and details. Obnoxiously opinionated but quietly generous.

And think about this: We are all beggars. We all sing for our supper. Sometimes we tap dance.

Have you seen CNBC's *Shark Tank*? Even entrepreneurs beg for business, investors, and opportunities. Sales types beg to close deals.

Farmers beg for rain. Sometimes they plead for the rain to stop. Commercial fishermen beg for a bountiful catch. Employees beg for jobs. Businesses and professionals beg for customers and clients. Artists beg for patrons. Beginners beg for a break. A chance. One succeeds; one doesn't. Some work harder. Some have more talent. Sometimes those who have the most talent self-destruct or are never discovered.

Others have better connections. They know the right people. Some parents introduce their children to the powerful. Some children don't know who their parents are.

Faced with a cop or a judge, we beg for mercy. Some students beg to make the team, to get into college, to get scholarships and grants. The sick and dying beg for miracles. The lonely beg for companionship.

We all need help in some way. We depend on the support of

others. Each of us is imperfect. Limited. Flawed. Scarred. But all of us are children of God. So beautifully human and unique, and like Jesus, made in the image and likeness of the divine. Imagine that. We're called to live up to that image.

And every one of us has a cross to bear. Unmistakably ours, like our fingerprints. There are those crosses we make for ourselves. Some we voluntarily pick up without realizing it. Even success can be a burden, too heavy for some to manage.

> "If anyone wishes to come after me, he must deny himself and take up his cross daily and follow me. For whoever wishes to save his life will lose it, but whoever loses his life for my sake will save it. What profit is there for one to gain the whole world yet lose or forfeit himself?" (Luke 9:23–25)

Jesus is "to die for"!

Our Lord is looking for cross carriers; people who are so grateful and in love with him they're also willing to help others carry their load. Even Jesus accepted assistance while lugging his cross up the hill. According to Matthew, Mark, and Luke, the Romans forced Simon of Cyrene to shoulder the wooden beam as he trudged along behind Jesus toward Calvary.

My cross might be shaped differently than yours, but it's heavy to me. Yet I can always find someone hauling around weightier issues. And often, the heavier the burden, the more grateful and graceful the laborer is who endures it.

If you help someone carry his or her cross, you'll find out how light yours is. Your perspective will change. You'll begin to discover that if you see the glass as half-full . . . it is. No recipe ever calls for a half-empty cup of anything. The half-full vessel is often sufficient. Christianity calls us to view life that way.

It's that simple and that hard.

Sharing crosses can lead to a deep realization that God is the reason for our true joy. Gratitude is humbling. It helps us forgive. Let go. Rejoice in the ordinary. Whenever I adopt an attitude of gratitude, I develop a desire to encounter God in order to say, "Thank you! I don't deserve your love—but I can't live without it." The *Catechism of the Catholic Church* says:

> The desire for God is written in the human heart, because man is created by God and for God; and God never ceases to draw man to himself. Only in God will he find the truth and happiness he never stops searching for. (*CCC*, 27)

Aren't we all dying to be happy? Whether we realize it or not, God is leading us to the ultimate homecoming we long to experience. A permanent dwelling in his house surrounded by his love. What a destination!

Along the way, he wants us to drop the noisy excesses of the flesh and pick up a quiet, spiritual glow in the here and now. And one day, like Jesus, we'll rise, transfigured, to live in the full light of God's glory and peace. Just as the Lord promised us. He will raise us up on the last day (see John 6:40).

Can you imagine heaven?

Quoting the Prophet Isaiah, Paul told the Corinthians that "eye has not seen, ear has not heard and human heart has not perceived what God has prepared for those who love him" (1 Corinthians 2:9). The lyrics of the requiem hymn, "In Paradisum," help us anticipate the red carpet reception we'll receive at the pearly gates. This is the final farewell chant the Church sings to her faithful, at the end of funeral Masses, complete with incense. What a send off, especially if you're ready to go—if you've fulfilled "The Sheep and the Goats Clause" and didn't step over poor Lazarus or your mother-in-law when they needed your mercy and love.

The Gregorian melody is as uplifting as the ancient words. Enjoy the ride:

> May the angels take you into paradise;
> may the martyrs come to welcome you on your way,
> and lead you into the holy city, Jerusalem.
> May the choir of angels welcome you;
> and with Lazarus who was once poor,
> may you have everlasting rest. [51]
> Amen.

Postscript

As I finish writing this book, Ellen has concluded her chemo treatments, and her hair is quickly growing back. She'll talk to the plastic surgeon about completing her breast reconstruction in a few months.

Our friend Betty qualified for a clinical trial that shrunk her tumors for a while. Unfortunately the therapy failed. Betty accepted God's will and made a pilgrimage to Lourdes, France. She gave us some water from the grotto there. Surrounded by family, Betty died just before Thanksgiving 2015.

We lost another friend to recurring breast cancer a few weeks later.

"Grandma Ellen" crocheted a beautiful raspberry-colored blanket for our first grandchild. While she was in the "chemo chair," she added a pink border. Our lovely granddaughter, Quinn Leigh Stepien, arrived August 9, 2015.

What a special joy it's been watching our older son, Alex, and his wife, Lauren, become parents.

Praise God for this day and his many blessings!

Acknowledgments

Thank you to all who prayed for us—and gave us so much love and support during Ellen's battle with breast cancer.

Your mercy brought us healing and the ever-present sense that God's arms are wrapped around us.

Notes

1. Vi-An Nguyen, "Songwriters Reveal the Story Behind 'Live Like You Were Dying' by Tim McGraw." *Parade* magazine, September 8, 2014; Athlon Media Group. http://parade. com/335635/viannguyen/songwriters-reveal-the-story -behind-live-like-you-were-dying-by-tim-mcgraw/.
2. Merriam-Webster Word Central, 2007. http://www .wordcentral.com/cgi-bin/student?book=Student&va =mercy+.
3. Compiled by José Luis González-Balado, *Mother Teresa In My Own Words* (New York: Gramercy Books, Random House, 1996) p.15.
4. Ibid., p. 50.
5. Ibid., p. 65.
6. Translated by Martha Vinson, *The Fathers of the Church, St. Gregory Nazianzus—Select Orations.* (Washington, D.C.: The Catholic University of America Press, 2003) p. 70.
7. Ibid., pp.70–71.
8. *Alcoholics Anonymous: The Story of How Many Thousands of Men and Women Have Recovered from Alcoholism, Fourth Edition* (New York: Alcoholics Anonymous World Services, Inc., 2001) p. 59.
9. *The Tools of Recovery: Helping Us Live and Work the Twelve Steps (pamphlet)* (Overeaters Anonymous, Inc., 2005) p. 2.

10. Dalai Lama, *The Path to Enlightenment* (Ithaca, NY: Snow Lions Publications Inc., 1982) p.114.

11. Translated by R. S. Pine-Coffin, *The Confessions, Vol. 16* (Penguin Classics, 1961), p.4.

12. Ibid.

13. *Alcoholics Anonymous*, p. 59.

14. Gerald G. May, M.D., *Addiction & Grace: Love and Spirituality in the Healing of Addictions* (New York: Harper Collins, 1988) pp. 38–39.

15. *Alcoholics Anonymous*, p.59.

16. Atul Gawande, MD, MPH, *Being Mortal: Illness, Medicine and What Happens in the End* (New York: Henry Holt and Company, 2014).

17. jesuitresource.org, "Easter Quotes." Xavier University's Center for Mission and Identity, 2015; http://www.xavier .edu/jesuitresource/online-resources/Easter.cfm.

18. Joseph Marquis and Chris Stepien, *Saint to Santa: How St. Nicholas Became Santa Claus* DVD (Boston: Pauline Books and Media, 2014).

19. Terry Matz, "St. Francis of Assisi." Catholic Online, 1996; http://www.catholic.org/saints/saint.php?saint_id=50.

20. Diane M. Houdek, "Married to Lady Poverty" American Catholic, 2013 http://www.americancatholic.org/Francis /Sections/FollowFrancis.aspx?id=56.

21. Matz, "St. Francis of Assisi."

22. World Meeting of Families, 2015; http://www.worldmeeting 2015.org/spirituality-center/ss-family/st-francis-assisi/.

23. Translated by Paschal Robinson, *The Writings of St. Francis of Assisi* (Philadelphia: The Dolphin Press, 1905).

24. "Saint Francis Quote of the Week." The National Shrine of St. Francis of Assisi Bulletin, March 8, 2015; http://www.shrinesf.org/Downloads/Bulletin-03-08-15.pdf.

25. "St. Elizabeth of Hungary." *New Advent Catholic Encyclopedia*, 2012; http://www.newadvent.org/cathen/05389a.htm.

26. Steve Hartman, *"Why a star football player traded NFL career for a tractor."* CBS News "On the Road"(2014); http://www.cbsnews.com/news/former-nfl-player-farms-for-good/; Tony Manfred, "Ex-NFL Player Who Made $25 Million Quit Football at Age 29 to Become a Farmer." *Business Insider*, November 2014; http://www.business insider.com/jason-brown-quit-football-farmer-2014-11.

27. Trent Beattie,"From Merciless Linebacker to Merciful Messenger: Eric Mahl of the Cleveland Browns was transformed by God's forgiving love." *National Catholic Register*, December 24, 2013; http://www.ncregister.com/daily-news/from-merciless-linebacker-to-merciful-messenger#ixzz3RfDo 6lHT. Note: Mahl's complete interview appears in *Fit for Heaven* by Trent Beattie (North Palm Beach, Fla.: Beacon Publishing, 2015) pp. 78–86.

28. Ibid.

29. Ibid.

30. Ibid.

31. Ibid.

32. Ibid.

33. Freddie Power, *Video from the Streets;* Keeping Hope Alive Ministries, 2011; http://keepinghopealiveministries.org/homeless-ministry/.

34. Ibid.

35. Ibid.

36. Efrem Graham, "Modern Day 'Mother Teresa' Heads Homeless Church." The Christian Broadcasting Network, July 2013; http://www.cbn.com/cbnnews/us/2013/July/Modern -Day-Mother-Theresa-Heads-Church-for-Homeless/.

37. *The Society of St. Vincent de Paul, What It Is…What It Does…* Council of the United States, Society of St. Vincent de Paul, St. Louis, Missouri. (2000) pp. 10, 15; "Blessed Frédéric Ozanam." American Catholic (1996–2015) http://www .americancatholic.org/features/saints/saint.aspx?id=1131.

38. *The Society of St. Vincent de Paul,* p. 15.

39. *United States Manual of the Society of St. Vincent de Paul—150th National Anniversary Commemorative Issue.* Council of the United States, Society of St. Vincent de Paul (1995) p. 8; Shaun McCarty S.T., "Frederick Ozanam: Lay Evangelizer." *Vincentian Heritage Journal,* DePaul University, University Libraries, 1996; pp. 8, 11, 12, 15;

40. "Ozanam, Antoine Frédéric," *The New Enclyclopaedia Britannica,* Vol. 9 (Chicago: The University of Chicago, 1993) pp.38–39. *United States Manual of the Society of St. Vincent de Paul,* p. 10.

41. *Rules and Commentaries—Society of St. Vincent de Paul.* Council of the United States, Society of St. Vincent de Paul, St. Louis, Missouri, 1980; p. 4

42. Frederic Ozanam Prayer Card, Society of St. Vincent de Paul

43. *Rules and Commentaries,* p. 5.

44. *Anxiety, Fear and Trust—Spiritual Readings for Conference Meetings.* Council of the United States, Society of St.

Vincent de Paul (Green Bay, Wisc.: Alt Publishing Company, 1989) p. 38.

45. Acoustic Nation, "Kansas' Kerry Livgren Shares the Story Behind 'Dust In The Wind.'" Guitar World; http://www .guitarworld.com/acoustic-nation-kansas-ken-livgren-shares -story-behind-dust-wind; Bruce Pollack, "Kerry Livgren of Kansas" and "Dust in the Wind." Song Facts, LLC; http:// www.songfacts.com/detail.php?id=380.

46. Sister Helen Prejean, *Dead Man Walking: The Eyewitness Account of the Death Penalty that Sparked a National Debate* (New York: Vintage Books, 1993); taken from the summary at amazon.com; http://www.amazon.com/Dead-Man -Walking-Eyewitness-National/dp/0679751319.

47. Edmund Miller, Guadalupe Partners, "Sidewalk Counseling." A speech presented at the National Sidewalk Counseling Symposium, August 8–9, 2014; www.GuadalupePartners.org.

48. Guadalupe Workers newsletter, March 2015 and June 2015; http://www.guadalupepartners.org/documents/2015/5 /March%202015%20newsletter%20.pdf.

49. "A Jew Looks at Christian Bible Studies." The Shap Working Party on World Religions in Education, 2015; London, England. http://www.shapworkingparty.org.uk/special edition/17_maccoby.html.

50. *Baltimore Catechism*, Lesson One, Question 150; http:// www.baltimore-catechism.com/lesson1.htm.

51. http://www.saintmeinrad.edu/media/55810/singing.pdf.

About the Author

As a journalist, Chris Stepien has spent his career asking tough questions and telling intriguing stories. He worked as a television producer-director and writer for the American Broadcasting Company (ABC). From 1979 to 1987, while at WXYZ-TV, Detroit, he won six Emmy* Awards and other honors for documentaries, sports and celebrity specials, and children's programming.

Stepien left broadcasting to co-found Adventure, Inc., a successful Detroit-based video/film production company. He created award-winning communications for Fortune 500 companies like General Motors and Ford Motor Company for nearly nine years.

Since 1996 Stepien has crafted marketing and advertising for global clients, as writer-creative director and owner of Stepien Creative Services, Inc.

A lifelong metro Detroiter and Catholic, Stepien attended parochial schools and was an altar boy. He and his wife, Ellen, have two adult sons, Alex and Mike. Stepien's first literary effort was a biblical novel about twelve-year-old Jesus, *Three Days: The Search for the Boy Messiah,* published by Beacon Publishing in 2015.

Share Your Thoughts

If you have questions or feedback about *Dying to Be Happy,* or would like to schedule an author talk, please write Chris Stepien at stepienwrites@gmail.com. Join the conversation at www.facebook.com/DyingToBeHappy/